'A Close Look At Unseen

by Rosemary Westwell

© R. J. Westwell 2014

"Genuine poetry can communicate before it is understood."

T.S. Eliot

https://www.goodreads.com/quotes/tag/poetry

CONTENTS

	Page
Introduction	5
What kind of poem is it?	6
How to describe the structure	8
The fine detail: A close look at rhythm and rhyme	9
Quiz 1 (Basic) What kind of poem is it?	11
Answers: What kind of poem is it?	12
Quiz 2 (Mammoth) What kind of poem is it?	14
Answers: What kind of poem is it?	18
A close look at poetry techniques (sometimes called 'poetic devices')	19
Quiz 3 (Basic) Poetry techniques	23
Answers: Poetry techniques	24
Quiz 4 (Mammoth) Poetry techniques	26
Answers: Poetry techniques	29
A close look at Humour	32
Quiz 5 Humour	33
Answers Humour	34
A-Z of poets and/or poems with analyses	36
Allingham, William 'Robin Redbreast'	36
Browning, Elizabeth 'How do I love thee?'	41
Clare, John 'I am'	44
Donne, John 'Death be not proud'	48
Eliot, T. S. Prelude 1 'The winter evening …'	51
'Full fathom five' by William Shakespeare	54
Gay, John 'The Butterfly and the Snail'	56
Heaney, Seamus ('Digging' – analysis only)	60
'If' by Rudyard Kipling	65
Joyce, James 'Strings in the Earth and Air'	70
Keats, John 'The Terror of Death'	72
Longfellow, Henry 'The Wreck of the Hesperus'	78
Milton, John 'Song on May morning'	88
Nashe, Thomas ''Spring, the sweet Spring'	89

Owen, Wilfred 'Anthem for a doomed youth'   91

Poe, Edgar Allen 'Sonnet – Silence'   94

'Queen Mab' by William Shakespeare   96

Rossetti, Christina Georgina 'Remember'   99

Shelley, Percy Bysshe 'The Widow Bird'   102

Tennyson, Alfred, Lord 'The Charge of the Light Brigade'   103

'Up, up up!' the first line of 'Choral Song of Illyrian peasants'   109
by Samuel Taylor Coleridge

'Violets' by John Moultrie   111

Wordsworth, William 'Daffodils'   112

Xuân Hương, Hồ 'Autumn Landscape'   115

Yeats, William Butler 'A Poet to his Beloved'   117

'Zermatt to the Matterhorn' by Thomas Hardy   119

'Poetry is the rhythmical creation of beauty in words.'

Edgar Allan Poe

https://www.goodreads.com/quotes/tag/poetry

Introduction

This book is written as support material for those studying for exams that contain unseen poems for analysis.

It offers an antidote to the more formal resources generally available by encouraging students to become involved in the mechanisms of poetry and by offering an A-Z of well-known poets or poems that provide essential background information.

A personal interpretation and analysis of each poem is included which is not meant to be a final, definitive account, but to provide a foundation from which students may develop their own powers of interpretation and analysis.

The book can also be used as a reference from cover to cover; teachers may dip into its contents to provide material for use in class, or they may use it as a quick reference for topics that need covering.

This resource may also be used by students for self-study. They may select particular poems for creating their own material in preparation for examinations or they may choose to use the quizzes as introductions to the subject, to test their knowledge or for revision.

Dr Rosemary Westwell *(PhD, MA (Ed), MA (TESOL), B Mus, BA (Hons)*
(rjwestwell@hotmail.com)

Do you daydream?

When you see a spectacular scene or picture, do you sometimes stop and think 'That's amazing!' and want to share this with someone so that they, too, can experience such wonder?

Do certain words or phrases bring a vivid image into your mind?
Then you already know what poets and poetry are about. You know what to look for:

Questions to ask when analysing a poem:

What is the poet trying to say, what is the poem's message?
How does the poet convey this message?

In more detail:

What kind of poem is it?

Note: many poems will not be one kind of poem or another, but may have attributes of one or more types or styles. When discussing poetry, you can say, for example, that the poem is like that of the Romantic poets.

Is it a lyric poem that reveals what the poet is thinking and feeling?
Is it Romantic poetry that contains personal, emotional language especially about the beauty of the world around us or about love?
Is it an example of Metaphysical poetry? Does it dwell on the magnificence of the universe, infinity and/or man's undefeatable spirit?
Is it a mystic poem that reaches beyond our normal consciousness?
Is it an intellectual poem that displays the poet's skill with words and the shape of the poem?
Is it comical? Does it try to make you laugh?
Is it tragic? Does it make you cry?
Is it a narrative poem that tells a story?
Is it an instructive poem that has a lesson for us to learn?

Is it a moralizing poem that exhorts its readers to be good and shun evil?

Is it a fanciful poem that stretches our imagination to the limit?

Is it a symbolic or 'allegorical' poem about something real that represents a much deeper element, for example a dove that symbolises peace?

Is it a monologue in which a particular character is speaking?

Does the poem sound like a letter? Is it an epistle poem?

Is it a burlesque that treats a serious subject humorously?

Is it high burlesque that takes something unimportant and makes it out to be very important?

Is it low burlesque that takes something important and makes it out to be unimportant?

Is it a Carpe Diem poem that is about living for today?

Is it a classical poem that relates to the ideals of beauty?

Is it doggerel or unliterary humorous verse?

Is it an elegy that expresses grief over the death of someone?

Is it an epic or a long serious poem that tells the story of a heroic figure?

Is it an epigram that is very short, ironic and witty?

Is it an epitaph that is a commemorative inscription on a tomb?

Is it an epithalamium (epithalamion) that praises a bride and groom at a wedding?

Is it an Idyll (Idyl) that depicts a peaceful country scene or is a long poem telling a story about heroes of long ago?

Is it a 'lay' poem or a long mediaeval sung poem that tells a story?

Is it an ode that is a long lyric poem?

Is it a pastoral poem about peaceful and romantic country life?

Is it a pindaric ode, a ceremonious poem that is balanced with question and answer-type lines?

(This list is not complete; try to add to this list as you practise analysing the poems).

_____

_____

_____

_____

_____

How is the poem structured?

Is the poem long or short?

How many lines does it have?

How are these lines grouped?

What is the main rhythm?

Does this rhythm change and if so why?

What is the rhyme scheme?

Does this vary and if so, why?

Structure Name:

Is it an ABC poem that has lines that begin with letters of the alphabet?

Is it an acrostic poem in which the first letter of each line spells a word?

Is it anapaest poem that uses the pattern of two short + one long syllable?

Is it a ballade (not to be confused with a ballad) that has 3 verses and an envoy (a short concluding verse) that have a specific rhyme?

Is it blank verse that is in iambic pentameter (5 groups of one short weak+ two long syllables) without rhymes?

Is it a 'Canzone' or a song with 5-6 stanzas and an envoy?

Is it a cinquain with five lines that increases or lowers the number of words in each line?

Is it a couplet or a poem of 2 lines that may or may not rhyme?

Is it dactyl poetry that uses the pattern one long + two short syllables?

Is it free verse (vers libre) that has no fixed metrical pattern?

Is it 'Found' poetry that re-arranges words, phrases, and passages from other sources?

Is it a Haiku that has three lines with 5+7+5 short syllables that do not rhyme?

Is it a Horatian ode that is a short lyric poem in two or four-line verses?

Is it a limerick that is a short humorous poem consisting of five anapaestic (two short followed by one long syllable) lines?

Is it a memoriam stanza that has four lines in iambic tetrameter: ABBA?

Is it Name poetry that uses the letters of a key word for the first letter of each line?

Is it a Petrarchan poem or a 14-line sonnet of 8 + 6 lines?

Is it a pindaric ode or a ceremonious poem that is balanced with question and answer-type lines?

Is it a quatrain that is a verse (stanza) or poem of four lines?

Is it a rondeau or a lyrical poem of 10 or 13 lines with a repeated refrain?

Is it a Sestina or a poem of six verses with six lines each and an 'envoy' of three lines?

Is it a sonnet or a lyric poem that consists of 14 lines with a special rhyming scheme?

Is it an Italian sonnet with 14 lines: 8 + 6?

Is it a Shakespearean or English sonnet or a lyric poem of 14 lines 4+4+4+2?

Is it sound poetry or 'verse without words'?

Is it a Tanka or a Japanese poem of five lines of 5+7+5+7+7 syllables?

Is it Terza Rima or a type of poetry of three-line 'tercets' of 10 or 11 syllables?

Is it a Villanelle or a 19-line poem 3+3+3+3+3+4 with a special rhyme pattern?

Is it 'Visual' or 'Concrete' poetry in which the meaning comes from the way the words are arranged on the page?

The fine detail: A close look at rhythm and rhyme

Rhythm

All language, including poetry, contains an underlying rhythm: some sounds are longer and more strongly emphasized than others. In poetry, the rhythm relates to how these stronger, longer sounds are combined with the shorter, weaker sounding ones. The stronger syllables in the rhythm of a poem are usually marked with an accent and the weaker ones are marked with a small 'u' above them as shown in the first letter of the common saying: 'ăn ápple a dáy keeps the dóctor awáy.'

Metre

In poetry, the rhythm is often grouped into metres, each metre consisting of a pattern of a particular 'foot' such as a weak syllable followed by a strong syllable (an 'iambic' foot). If the weak/strong pattern is repeated five times it is said to be iambic pentameter. ('Penta' means 'five' as in the word 'pentagon').   For example, the opening line of 'Twelfth Night' by William Shakespeare: 'If músic bé the fóod of lóve play ón.' u/u/u/u/u/ or 'dee dum, dee dum, dee dum, dee dum, dee dum' (= five repetitions of the pattern of a weak syllable followed by a strong one = five 'feet').

Different meters:

A line of one foot = a monometer

A line of two feet = a dimeter

A line of three feet = a trimeter

A line of four feet = a tetrameter

A line of five feet = pentameter

A line of six feet = hexameter

A line of seven feet = a heptameter

A line of eight feet = an octameter

Rhyme

When the same sounds occur closely together, the words that contain these sounds are said to rhyme. In 'an apple a day keeps the doctor away' the vowels in 'd<u>a</u>y' and 'aw<u>ay</u>' sound the same, i.e. the two words 'rhyme'. Note: words that appear to have the same vowels but that are not pronounced the same do not 'rhyme' e.g. 'way' and 'weigh' rhyme; whereas 'weight' and 'height' do not.

'Roses are red,

Violets are blue …

Whatever is read/ fed? / shed? / said?

I love Sue? / too? / to woo? / you?'

Quiz 1:

(Basic) What do you know about poetry? What kind of poem is it?

Choose from the following to complete the list below to fill the gaps:

ABC, epigram, ballad, burlesque, Carpe Diem, couplet, doggerel, elegy, acrostic, Classicism, free verse, Haiku, sonnet, limerick, blank verse, epic, lyric, narrative, ode, pastoral, epitaph, Romanticism

e.g. An ABC poem has lines that begin with letters of the alphabet

In an _acrostic_ poem, the first letter of each line spells a word.

Ballad
narrative tells a story.

blank verse is poetry in iambic pentameter written without rhymes.

Burlesque treats a serious subject humorously.

Carpe diem poems are about living for today.

Classicism is a style that relates to the ideals of beauty.

Couplet is a poem of 2 lines that may or may not rhyme.

Doggerel is 'cheap' or unliterary humorous verse.

Elegy expresses grief over the death of someone.

Epic is a long serious poem that tells the story of a heroic figure.

Epigram is very short, ironic and witty.

Epitaph is a commemorative inscription on a tomb.

Free Vers has no fixed metrical pattern.

Haiku has three lines with 5+7+5 short syllables that do not rhyme.

Limerick is a short humorous poem consisting of five anapaestic lines.

Lyric poem is often a sonnet and expresses the thoughts and feelings of the poet.

Narrative poem is one that tells a story e.g. ballads, epics and lays.

Ode is a long lyric poem.

Pastoral poem is about country life which it describes as peaceful and romantic.

Romantic is about personal experience of nature and love.

A Sonnet is a lyric poem that consists of 14 lines with a special rhyming scheme.

Answers:

e.g. An _ABC_ poem has lines that begin with letters of the alphabet.

In an _acrostic_ poem, the first letter of each line spells a word.

A _ballad_ tells a story.

Blank verse is poetry in iambic pentameter written without rhymes.

Burlesque treats a serious subject humorously.

Carpe Diem poems are about living for today.

Classicism is a style that relates to the ideals of beauty.

A _couplet_ is a poem of 2 lines that may or may not rhyme.

Doggerel is 'cheap' or unliterary humorous verse.

An _elegy_ expresses grief over the death of someone.

An _epic_ is a long serious poem that tells the story of a heroic figure.

An _epigram_ is very short, ironic and witty.

An _epitaph_ is a commemorative inscription on a tomb.

Free verse (vers libre) has no fixed metrical pattern.

Haiku has three lines with 5+7+5 short syllables that do not rhyme.

A *limerick* is a short humorous poem consisting of five anapaestic lines.

A *lyric* poem is often a sonnet and expresses the thoughts and feelings of the poet.

A *narrative* poem is one that tells a story e.g. ballads, epics and lays.

An *ode* is a long lyric poem.

A *pastoral* poem is about country life which it describes as peaceful and romantic.

Romanticism is about personal experience of nature and love.

A *sonnet* is a lyric poem that consists of 14 lines with a special rhyming scheme.

If you think you know it all, try this quiz:

Quiz 2

<u>(Mammoth) What do you know about poetry? What kind of poem is it?</u>

Choose from the following to complete the list below:

ABC, acrostic, An analogue, a ballad, blank verse, cacophony, a carpe diem poem, Classicism, a couplet, dactyl poetry, an epigram, an epithalamium, free verse, a ghazal, Haiku, a cinquain, high burlesque, an Horatian ode, Idyll (Idyl) poetry, an Italian sonnet, a 'lay' poem, a limerick, low burlesque, a lyric poem, burlesque, a memoriam stanza, found poetry, Name poetry, a narrative poem, Anapaest poetry, an ode, a pastoral poem, Conceit, a Petrarchan poem, a quatrain, Romanticism, doggerel, a ballade, a rondeau, a senryu, an elegy, a sestina, a Shakespearean or English sonnet, a sonnet, a 'canzone', a pindaric ode, sound poetry, a Tanka, an epitaph, Terza Rima, A Villanelle, an epic, 'Visual' or 'Concrete' poetry

e.g. An *ABC* poem has lines that begin with letters of the alphabet

_____ poem, the first letter of each line spells a word.

_____ compares two things that are unalike.

_____ poetry has lines of the pattern two short + one long syllable.

_____ tells a story.

_____ has 3 verses and an envoy that has a specific rhyme.

_____ is poetry in iambic pentameter written without rhymes

_____ treats a serious subject humorously.

_____ uses sharp, harsh, hissing or discordant sounds to make up a poem.

_____ means 'song' in Italian and has 5-6 stanzas and an envoy.

_____ poems are about living for today.

_____ is a poem of five lines that increases or lowers the words per line.

_____ is a style that relates to the ideals of beauty.

_____ likens something to something else that is very different.

_____ is a poem of 2 lines that may or may not rhyme.

_____ has lines of the pattern: one long + two short syllables.

_____ is 'cheap' or unliterary humorous verse.

_____ expresses grief over the death of someone.

_____ is a long serious poem that tells the story of a heroic figure.

_____ is very short, ironic and witty.

_____ is a commemorative inscription on a tomb.

_____ praises a bride and groom at a wedding.

_____ (vers libre) has no fixed metrical pattern.

_____ poetry re-arranges words, phrases, and passages from other sources.

_____ is a short poem in Urdu from 5 to 15 couplets long.

_____ has three lines with 5+7+5 short syllables that do not rhyme.

_____ takes something unimportant but makes it out to be very important.

_____ is a short lyric poem in two or four-line verses.

_____ poetry depicts a peaceful country scene or is a long poem telling a story about heroes of long ago.

_____ has 14 lines: 8 + 6.

'_____ is a long mediaeval sung poem that tells a story.

_____ is a short humorous poem consisting of five anapaestic lines.

_____ takes something important and makes it out to be unimportant.

_____ is often a sonnet and expresses the thoughts and feelings of the poet.

_____ has four lines in iambic tetrameter: ABBA.

_____ is poetry using the letters of a key word for the first letter of each line.

_____ is one that tells a story e.g. ballads, epics and lays.

_____ is a long lyric poem.

_____ is about country life which it describes as peaceful and romantic.

_____ is a 14-line sonnet of 8 + 6 lines.

_____ is a ceremonious poem that is balanced with question and answer lines.

_____ is a verse (stanza) or poem of four lines.

_____ is about personal experience of nature and love.

_____ is a lyrical poem of 10 or 13 with a repeated refrain.

_____ is a short humorous or satirical Japanese-style poem.

_____ is a poem of six verses with six lines each and an 'envoy' of three lines.

_____ is a lyric poem of 14 lines 4+4+4+2.

_____ is a lyric poem that consists of 14 lines with a special rhyming scheme.

_____ poetry is poetry without words.

_____ is a Japanese poem of five lines, 5+7+5+7+7 syllables.

_____ is a type of poetry of three-line 'tercets' of 10 or 11 syllables.

_____ is a 19-line poem 3+3+3+3+3+4 with a special rhyme pattern.

_____ poetry, the meaning comes from the way the words are arranged on the page.

Answers:

e.g. An *ABC* poem has lines that begin with letters of the alphabet

In an *acrostic* poem, the first letter of each line spells a word.

An *analogue* compares two things that are unalike.

Anapaest poetry uses the pattern: two short + one long syllable.

A *ballad* tells a story.

A *ballade* has 3 verses and an envoy that have a specific rhyme.

Blank verse is poetry in iambic pentameter written without rhymes.

Burlesque treats a serious subject humorously.

Cacophony uses sharp, harsh, hissing or discordant sounds to make up a poem.

'Canzone' means 'song' in Italian and has 5-6 stanzas and an envoy.

Carpe Diem poems are about living for today.

A *cinquain* is a poem in five lines that increase or lower the words per line.

Classicism is a style that relates to the ideals of beauty.

Conceit likens something to something else that is very different.

A *couplet* is a poem of 2 lines that may or may not rhyme.

Dactyl poetry uses the pattern: one long + two short syllables.

Doggerel is 'cheap' or unliterary humorous verse.

An *elegy* expresses grief over the death of someone.

An *epic* is a long serious poem that tells the story of a heroic figure.

An *epigram* is very short, ironic and witty.

An *epitaph* is a commemorative inscription on a tomb.

An *epithalamium* (epithalamion) praises a bride and groom at a wedding.

Free verse (vers libre) has no fixed metrical pattern.

Found poetry re-arranges words, phrases, and passages from other sources.

A *ghazal* is a short poem Urdu from 5 to 15 couplets long.

Haiku has three lines with 5+7+5 short syllables that do not rhyme.

High burlesque takes something unimportant makes it out to be very important.

An *Horatian ode* is a short lyric poem in two or four-line verses.

*Idyll (*Idyl) poetry depicts a peaceful country scene or is a long poem telling a story about heroes of long ago.

An *Italian sonnet* has 14 lines: 8 + 6.

A *'lay'* poem is a long mediaeval sung poem that tells a story.

A *limerick* is a short humorous poem consisting of five anapaestic lines.

Low burlesque takes something important and makes it out to be unimportant.

A *lyric* poem is often a sonnet and expresses the thoughts and feelings of the poet.

A *memoriam stanza* has four lines in iambic tetrameter: ABBA.

Name poetry uses the letters of a key word for the first letter of each line.

A *narrative* poem is one that tells a story e.g. ballads, epics and lays.

An *ode* is a long lyric poem.

A *pastoral* poem is about country life which it describes as peaceful and romantic.

A *Petrarchan* poem is a 14-line sonnet of 8 + 6 lines.

A *pindaric ode* is a ceremonious poem that is balanced with question and answer-type lines.

A *quatrain* is a verse (stanza) or poem of four lines.

Romanticism is about personal experience of nature and love.

A *rondeau* is a lyrical poem of 10 or 13 with a repeated refrain.

A *senryu* is a short humorous or satirical Japanese-style poem.

A *Sestina* is a poem of six verses with six lines each and an 'envoy' of three lines.

Shakespearean or *English sonnet* is a lyric poem of 14 lines 4+4+4+2.

A *sonnet* is a lyric poem that consists of 14 lines with a special rhyming scheme.

Sound poetry is poetry without words.

A *Tanka* is a Japanese poem of five lines, 5+7+5+7+7 syllables.

Terza Rima is a type of poetry of three-line 'tercets' of 10 or 11 syllables.

A *Villanelle* is a 19-line poem 3+3+3+3+3+4 with a special rhyme pattern.

In *'Visual'* or *'Concrete'* poetry, the meaning comes from the way the words are arranged on the page.

Close look at poetry techniques (sometimes called 'poetic devices')

Alliteration: words that begin with the same letter, e.g. Two toads were totally tired.

Assonance: contains the same vowel sounds, e.g. the half-heard word stirred.

Cohesion: joining aspects of the poem so that the whole poem is 'one' expression or idea, often by constant or regular references to particular sounds, assonances, or alliterations in different parts of the poem.

Collocation/ Implied Collocation: 'the tall building', 'the high building', 'the tall man' are phrases which contain words that are often associated together, but 'the high man' is seldom used as 'high' is not usually associated (or collocated) with 'man' (depending on context). We may think of common collocations with a word or words in the poem that are not present but may be implied by the context.

Comparison/ Simile: The thief was as cunning as a fox.

Connotations / Implied Connotations: (associated meanings) for example the word 'fly' may remind us of the phrase 'fly high' or 'do well', or fly away : - run away, or escape. Alternatively, depending on the situation or 'context', we may be reminded of a wish to be a 'fly on the wall' to hear or see something that we would not expect to be able to.

Contrast: He was as clumsy as a drunken tramp. She was as dainty as a cat.

Euphemism: hints at a harsh truth, such as saying 'He passed away,' instead of 'He died'.

Enjambment: continuing a line into the next one without a break sometimes in order to give more weight or importance to the idea(s) expressed.

Figurative language: has a hidden meaning, e.g. he has a finger in every pie meaning he is involved in many different activities.

Grammar: use of specific grammatical structures for emphasis, for example in the line 'The free bird leaps', the poet uses 'the' instead of 'a', meaning that 'the free bird' mentioned in the poem is not one bird, but represents all types of free birds.

Common grammar constructions:

1. Use of the article: a, the, or no article, for example
   - <u>a</u> book (we don't know which one)
   - <u>the</u> book on the table (we know which one – the one on the table)
   - <u>Books</u> are found in most homes. (We don't know how many –'books' has a general meaning – 'books everywhere').

2. Use of verb tense: We go to school (present simple – we do it every day, often)
   - We are going to school (present continuous – we are doing it NOW or we have decided to do it in the future.)
   - They have gone to catch the bus for school – present perfect = happens in the past just before the present

- We were going to school when the bus arrived = past continuous - happens in the past before something else in the past, or when interrupted by something else in the past.
- We went to school – past simple = it happened in the past and the action is finished
- We had gone to school – past perfect = it happened in the past before something else in the past.

3. Participles: the past participle - He has <u>gone</u>.

                                     the present participle - He is <u>running</u>.

4. Active Voice: e.g. The boy closed the door. The subject, or most important noun, comes first and does the action. In the passive voice, for example: The door was closed by the boy. The importance of the nouns is changed and the object, the door, becomes more important and is mentioned first. The subject (the boy) still does the action, but is mentioned last.

5. Preposition: He went <u>to</u> the shops.

6. Spelling: use of unusual spelling perhaps to create dialect (a special form of a language e.g. English, the use of slang in a London dialect e.g. gisit = give us it, or in more formal English 'give it to us').

7. Punctuation:

- Full stop (.) ends a sentence, a line, an idea or a stanza or ends a shortened word such as Oct.
- Comma (,) separates words, clauses, phrases or ideas.
- Semi-colon (;) separates clauses closely connected with each other.
- Colon (:) introduces speech or a list.
- Question mark (?) is put at the end of a question or indicates the poet is asking a question, is uncertain or challenges something.
- Apostrophe (') shows possession e.g. the boy's book, the boys' books, the children's books.

- Inverted commas ('' or "") show actual words spoken or written.
- Rounded brackets () show words that have been added or are not important to the whole meaning of the phrase/clause.
- Conjunctions: join ideas e.g. 'and', 'but', 'however, 'although'.

8. Hyperbole: exaggeration, e.g. I drank gallons of lemonade.

9. Imagery: uses words that appeal to the senses: sight sound, touch, smell or taste, e.g. the rosy clouds.

10. Literal use of words: e.g. He put his finger into the pie to taste it.

11. Litotes: under-statement e.g. He passed with 100 per cent, so he knows a little of his subject.

12. Metaphor: The man was a fox.

13. Onomatopoeia: words sound like the sounds they represent e.g. squelching footsteps.

14. Paradox: something true which appears to be a contradiction, e.g. The truer the statement, the more it is disbelieved.

15. Personification, like human beings, e.g. The flowers danced.

Quiz 3

(Basic) Poetry techniques

Choose from the following to fill the gaps:

alliteration, assonance, cohesion, collocation, simile, connotations, contrast, euphemism, enjambment, figurative language, article, dialect, hyperbole, imagery,literal,litotes,metaphor,onomatopoeia,paradox,personification

For example: assonance *contains the same vowel sounds - the half-heard word stirred*

collocation   words that are often associated together e.g. the tall building

Idioms   e.g. to be 'fed up' means to be tired of something (not to be full from eating as much as we can.)

simile   For example - The thief was as cunning as a fox.

connotation   meaning of the word in context e.g. the word 'fly' may remind us of an insect or what an aeroplane does.

alliteration   words that begin with the same letter e.g. Two toads were totally tired.

figurative   has a hidden meaning e.g. he has a finger in every pie, meaning he is involved in many different activities

cohesion   joining aspects of the poem so that the whole poem is 'one'.

dialect   a special form of a language e.g. East London slang

contrast   e.g. He was as clumsy as a drunken tramp. She was as dainty as a cat.

Imagery   uses words that appeal to the senses such as 'the rosy clouds'

enjambment?   continuing a line into the next one without a break

literal   use of words e.g. He put his finger into the pie to taste it.

litotes   under-statement e.g. He passed with 100 per cent so he knows a little of his subject.

metaphor   e.g. The man was a fox.

paradox   something true that appears to be a contradiction e.g. The truer the statement the more it is disbelieved.

euphemism   hints at a harsh truth e.g. saying 'He passed away.' instead of 'He died.'

personification   like human beings e.g. The flowers danced.

hyperbole   exaggerates e.g. I drank gallons of lemonade.

onomatopoeia   words sound like the sounds they represent e.g. squelching footsteps

article   a or the.

Answers

Choose from the following to fill the gaps: idioms and implied idioms …

<u>*For example assonance*</u> *contains the same vowel sounds. - the half-heard word stirred.*

Collocation: words that are often associated together e.g. the tall building.

Idioms /implied idioms / sayings: to be 'fed up' means to be tired of something (not to be full from eating as much as we can.)

Simile: The thief was as cunning as a fox.

Connotation: meaning of the word in context. e.g. the word 'fly' may remind us of an insect as well as what an aeroplane does.

Alliteration: words that begin with the same letter e.g. Two toads were totally tired.

Figurative language: has a hidden meaning e.g. he has a finger in every pie meaning he is involved in many different activities.

Cohesion: joining aspects of the poem so that the whole poem is 'one'.

Dialect: a special form of a language e.g. East London slang.

Contrast: He was as clumsy as a drunken tramp. She was as dainty as a cat.

Imagery: uses words that appeal to the senses sight sound touch smell or taste e.g. the rosy clouds.

Enjambment: continuing a line into the next one without a break.

Literal use of words: He put his finger into the pie to taste it.

Litotes: under-statement e.g. He passed with 100 per cent so he knows a little of his subject.

Metaphor: The man was a fox.

Paradox: something true which appears to be a contradiction e.g. The truer the statement the more it is disbelieved.

Euphemism: hints at a harsh truth e.g. saying 'He passed away.' instead of 'He died.'

Personification: like human beings e.g. The flowers danced.

Hyperbole: exaggerates e.g. I drank gallons of lemonade.

Onomatopoeia: words sound like the sounds they represent e.g. squelching footsteps

Article: a, the

Quiz 4

(Mammoth) Poetry techniques

Choose from the following to fill the gaps:

idioms and implied idioms or sayings, alliteration, assonance, cohesion, collocation, simile, connotations, contrast, euphemism, enjambment, figurative language, grammar, article, present simple, present continuous, present perfect, past continuous, past simple, past perfect, past participle, present participle, active voice, passive voice, preposition, dialect, full stop, comma, semi-colon, colon, question mark, apostrophe, inverted commas, rounded brackets, conjunctions, hyperbole, imagery, literal, litotes, metaphor, onomatopoeia, paradox, personification.

For example assonance contains the same vowel sounds - the half-heard word stirred.

Collocation — 'the tall building', 'the high building', 'the tall man' are phrases which contain words that are often associated together, but 'the high man' is seldom used, as 'high' is not usually associated or collocated with 'man' (depending on context). We may think of common collocations with a word or words in the poem that are not present but may be implied by the context.

idioms — e.g. the use of the word 'leaps' in 'The free bird leaps' brings to mind the common saying or 'idiom' of to 'leap for joy'. (Idioms are rarely literal, they have a special meaning associated with them e.g. we do not mean we jump up physically with joy. Another example of an idiom is: to be 'fed up' is to be tired of something (not to be full from eating as much as we can).

simile — The thief was as cunning as a fox.

past continuous — a verb tense e.g. We were going to school when the bus arrived - happens in the past before something else in the past, or when interrupted by something else in the past.

connotation — associated meaning e.g. the word 'fly' may remind us of the phrase 'fly high' or 'do well', or fly away - run away, or escape. Alternatively, depending on the situation or 'context', we may be reminded of a wish to be a 'fly on the wall' to hear or see something that we would not able to.

a verb tense, such as: They have gone to catch the bus for school - happens in the past just before the present.

hints at a harsh truth - saying 'He passed away' instead of 'He died'.

words that begin with the same letter, - Two toads were totally tired.

has a hidden meaning, e.g. he has a finger in every pie (meaning he is involved in many different activities).

grammar part of speech used to define a noun e.g. a, the

a verb tense e.g. We go to school (we do it every day/often).

e.g. He was as clumsy as a drunken tramp. She was as dainty as a cat.

grammar part of speech, the second part of a verb in the present e.g. He is running.

The boy closed the door. The subject, or most important noun, comes first and does the action. In the passive voice, e.g. The door was closed by the boy. The importance of the nouns is changed and the object, the door, becomes more important and is mentioned first. The subject (the boy) still does the action, but is mentioned last.

grammar part of speech joining 2 nouns e.g. He went to the shops.

joining aspects of the poem so that the whole poem is 'one' expression or idea, often by constant or regular references to particular sounds, assonances, or alliterations in different parts of the poem.

words sound like the sounds they represent e.g. squelching footsteps.

a special form of a language e.g. East London slang - 'gisit' not 'give us it'.

(.) punctuation mark that ends a sentence, a line, an idea or a stanza or ends a shortened word e.g. Oct.

(,) punctuation mark that separates words, clauses, phrases or ideas.

(;) separates clauses closely connected with each other.

() punctuation mark that introduces speech or a list.

(?) a punctuation mark that is put at the end of a question or indicates the poet is asking a questions, is uncertain or challenges something.

(') An apostrophe shows possession e.g. the boy's book, the boys' books, the children's books.

past perfect A verb tense e.g. We had gone to school – it happened in the past before something else in the past.

inverted commas ('and' or "and") punctuation marks that show actual words spoken or written.

rounded braces () punctuation marks that show words that have been added or are not important to the whole meaning of the phrase/clause.

conjunctions grammar part of speech that joins ideas e.g. 'and', 'but', 'however, 'although'.

hyperbole exaggerates, e.g. I drank gallons of lemonade.

present continuous a verb tense e.g. We are going to school (we are doing it NOW or we have decided to do it in the future).

imagery uses words that appeal to the senses sight sound, touch, smell or taste, e.g. the rosy clouds.

paradox something true which appears to be a contradiction, e.g. The truer the statement, the more it is disbelieved.

enjambment continuing a line into the next one without a break sometimes in order to give more weight or importance to the idea(s) expressed.

past simple a verb tense e.g. We went to school – it happened in the past and the action is finished.

figurative use of words e.g. He put his finger into the pie to taste it.

litotes under-statement e.g. He passed with 100 per cent, so he knows a little of his subject.

metaphor e.g. The man was a fox.

past participle grammar part of speech, the second part of a verb in the past e.g. He has <u>gone</u>.

Grammar use of specific structures for emphasis e.g. in a line 'The free bird leaps', the poet uses 'the' instead of 'a', meaning that 'the free bird' mentioned in the poem is not one bird, but represents all types of free birds.

personification like human beings, e.g. The flowers danced.

"Poetry, she thought, wasn't written to be analyzed; it was meant to inspire without reason, to touch without understanding."

Nicholas Sparks, The Notebook

https://www.goodreads.com/quotes/tag/poetry

Answers

Choose from the following to fill the gaps:
idioms and implied idioms or sayings, alliteration, assonance, cohesion, collocation, simile, connotations, contrast, euphemism, enjambment, figurative language, grammar, article, present simple, present continuous, present perfect, past continuous, past simple, past perfect, past participle, present participle, active voice, passive voice, preposition, dialect, full stop, comma, semi-colon, colon, question mark, apostrophe, inverted commas, rounded brackets, conjunctions, hyperbole, imagery, literal, litotes, metaphor, onomatopoeia, paradox, personification.

Assonance: contains the same vowel sounds, e.g. the half-heard word stirred.

Collocation/ Implied Collocation: 'the tall building', 'the high building', 'the tall man' are phrases which contain words that are often associated together i.e. they are common collocations – but 'the high man' is seldom used, 'high' is not usually associated or collocated with 'man' (depending on context). We may think of common collocations with a word or words in the poem that are not present but may be implied by the context.

Idioms / Implied Idioms / sayings: the use of the word 'leaps' in 'The free bird leaps' brings to mind the common saying or 'idiom' of to 'leap for joy'. (Idioms are rarely literal, they have a special meaning associated with them e.g. we do not mean we jump up physically with joy. Another example of an idiom is: to be 'fed up' is to be tired of something (not to be full from eating as much as we can).

Simile: The thief was as cunning as a fox.

Past Continuous: a verb tense e.g. We were going to school when the bus arrived - happens in the past before something else in the past, or when interrupted by something else in the past.

Connotation / Implied Connotations: associated meaning - the word 'fly' may remind us of the phrase 'fly high' or 'do well', or fly away - run away, or escape. Alternatively, depending on the situation or 'context', we may be reminded of a wish to be a 'fly on the wall' to hear or see something that we would not expect to be able to.

Present Perfect: a verb tense - They have gone to catch the bus for school = happens in the past just before the present.

Euphemism: hints at a harsh truth, e.g. saying 'He passed away.' instead of 'He died.'

Alliteration: words that begin with the same letter - Two toads were totally tired.

Figurative Language: has a hidden meaning, e.g. he has a finger in every pie meaning he is involved in many different activities.

Article: grammar part of speech used to define a noun e.g. a, the.

Present Simple: a verb tense e.g. We go to school (we do it every day/often).

Contrast: He was as clumsy as a drunken tramp. She was as dainty as a cat.

Present Participle: grammar part of speech, the second part of a verb in the present e.g. He is running.

Active Voice: The boy closed the door. The subject, or most important noun, comes first and does the action. In the passive voice, e.g. The door was closed by the boy. The importance of the nouns is changed and the object, the door, becomes more important and is mentioned first. The subject (the boy) still does the action, but is mentioned last.

Preposition: grammar part of speech joining 2 nouns e.g. *He* went to the *shops*.

Cohesion: joining aspects of the poem so that the whole poem is 'one' expression or idea, often by constant or regular references to particular sounds, assonances, or alliterations in different parts of the poem.

Onomatopoeia: words sound like the sounds they represent e.g. squelching footsteps.

Dialect: a special form of a language such as East London slang - 'gisit' not 'give us it'.

Full stop (.) ends a sentence, a line, an idea or a stanza or ends a shortened word e.g. Oct.

Comma (,) separates words, clauses, phrases or ideas.

Semi-colon (;) separates clauses closely connected with each other.

Colon (:) introduces speech or a list.

Question mark (?) is put at the end of a question or indicates the poet is asking a question, is uncertain or challenges something.

An apostrophe (') shows possession e.g. the boy's book, the boys' books, the children's books.

Past Perfect: a verb tense e.g. We had gone to school – it happened in the past before something else in the past.

Inverted Commas ('and' or "and") show actual words spoken or written.

Rounded Brackets () show words that have been added or are not important to the whole meaning of the phrase/clause.

Conjunction: grammar part of speech that joins ideas e.g. 'and', 'but', 'however, 'although'.

Hyperbole: exaggerates, e.g. I drank gallons of lemonade.

Present Continuous: a verb tense e.g. We are going to school (we are doing it NOW or we have decided to do it in the future).

Imagery: uses words that appeal to the senses sight sound, touch, smell or taste, e.g. the rosy clouds.

Paradox: something true which appears to be a contradiction, e.g. The truer the statement, the more it is disbelieved.

Enjambment: continuing a line into the next one without a break sometimes in order to give more weight or importance to the idea(s) expressed.

Past Simple: a verb tense e.g. We went to school – it happened in the past and the action is finished.

Literal: use of words e.g. He put his finger into the pie to taste it.

Litotes: under-statement e.g. He passed with 100 per cent, so he knows a little of his subject.

Metaphor: The man was a fox.

Past Participle: grammar part of speech, the second part of a verb in the past e.g. He has gone.

Grammar: use of specific structures for emphasis e.g. in a line 'The free bird leaps', the poet uses 'the' instead of 'a', meaning that 'the free bird' mentioned in the poem is not one bird, but represents all types of free birds.

Personification: like human beings, e.g. The flowers danced.

A close look at Humour

Black humour: deals with the unpleasant things of life in a bitter or ironic way, e.g. A man takes off his belt to hang himself. His trousers fall down.

Dry humour: someone with a dry sense of humour pretends to be serious when they are not, e.g. I see you've set aside this special time to humiliate yourself in public.

A Joke: something that makes people laugh, e.g. A man says he has a dog that plays the piano and a snake that sings. His mate challenges him. The dog and snake are brought in and the dog plays the piano while the snake sings. The mate is amazed and apologises. The man pauses saying he feels guilty. When asked why, he explains that the dog was a ventriloquist.

Idioms /Implied Idioms / Sayings: e.g. the use of the word 'leaps' in 'The free bird leaps' brings to mind the common saying or 'idiom' of to 'leap for joy'. (Idioms are rarely literal, they have a special meaning associated with them e.g. we do not mean we jump up physically with joy. Another example of an idiom is: to be 'fed up' is to be tired of something (not to be full from eating as much as we can).

Innuendo/Double Entendre: the speaker appears innocent but hidden within their speech is an indirect reference to something, e.g. Comedians do it standing up.

Irony: using words that are the opposite of what you really mean in order to be amusing, e.g. saying 'What a lovely day!' while walking through a hailstorm.

Parody: copying or mimicking something well known for comic effect, e.g. The ten commandments for cooks are...

Play on Words: using a word that is interesting or amusing because it has two very different meanings, e.g. patient: 'Doctor, doctor, I feel like a pair of curtains.' Doctor: 'Well pull yourself together!'

Pun: an amusing use of a word or phrase that has two meanings, e.g. Seven days without water can make one weak - 1 week.

Riddle: a question that is deliberately confusing and usually has a clever or humorous answer, e.g. What is black and white and red all over? Answer: an embarrassed zebra.

Sarcasm: a way of speaking or writing that involves saying the opposite of what you really mean in order to make an unkind joke, e.g. in response to someone arriving an hour late, someone says: 'Good of you to arrive on time.'

Satire: using humour to expose foolishness, silliness or stupidity through ridicule, e.g. The government has appointed a new minister: The Minister for Silly Walks.

Quiz 5

Humour

Chose from the following to fill the gaps
A joke, idioms and implied idioms or sayings, irony, a play on words, dry humour, a riddle, sarcasm, a pun, satire, innuendo/double entendre.

Black Humour deals with the unpleasant things of life in a bitter or ironic way, such as man takes off his belt to hang himself. His trousers fall down.

Dry — someone with a dry sense of humour pretends to be serious when they are not, e.g. I see you've set aside this special time to humiliate yourself in public.

Joke — something that makes people laugh, e.g. A man says he has a dog that plays the piano and a snake that sings. His mate challenges him. The dog and snake are brought in and the dog plays the piano while the snake sings. The mate is amazed and apologises. The man pauses saying he feels guilty. When asked why, he explains that the dog was a ventriloquist.

Innuendo — the speaker appears innocent but hidden within their speech is an indirect reference to something, e.g. Comedians do it standing up.

Irony — using words that are the opposite of what you really mean in order to be amusing, e.g. saying 'What a lovely day!' while walking through a hailstorm.

Parody — copying or mimicking something well known for comic effect, e.g. The ten commandments for cooks are...

play on words — using a word that is interesting or amusing because it has two very different meanings, e.g. patient 'Doctor, doctor, I feel like a pair of curtains.' Doctor 'Well pull yourself together!'

Pun — an amusing use of a word or phrase that has two meanings, e.g. Seven days without water can make one weak - 1 week.

riddle — a question that is deliberately confusing and usually has a clever or humorous answer, e.g. What is black and white and red all over? Answer an embarrassed zebra.

sarcasm — a way of speaking or writing that involves saying the opposite of what you really mean in order to make an unkind joke, e.g. in response to someone arriving an hour late, someone says 'Good of you to arrive on time.'

Satire — using humour to expose foolishness, silliness or stupidity through ridicule, e.g. The government has appointed a new minister The Minister for Silly Walks.

Answers

Chose from the following to fill the gaps:
A joke, idioms and implied idioms or sayings, irony, a play on words, dry humour, a riddle, sarcasm, a pun, satire, innuendo/double entendre.

Black Humour: deals with the unpleasant things of life in a bitter or ironic way, such as man takes off his belt to hang himself. His trousers fall down.

Dry Humour: someone with a dry sense of humour pretends to be serious when they are not, e.g. I see you've set aside this special time to humiliate yourself in public.

A Joke: something that makes people laugh, e.g. A man says he has a dog that plays the piano and a snake that sings. His mate challenges him. The dog and snake are brought in and the dog plays the piano while the snake sings. The mate is amazed and apologises. The man pauses saying he feels guilty. When asked why, he explains that the dog was a ventriloquist.

Innuendo/Double Entendre: the speaker appears innocent but hidden within their speech is an indirect reference to something, e.g. Comedians do it standing up.

Irony: using words that are the opposite of what you really mean in order to be amusing, e.g. saying 'What a lovely day!' while walking through a hailstorm.

Parody: copying or mimicking something well known for comic effect, e.g. The ten commandments for cooks are...

Play on Words: using a word that is interesting or amusing because it has two very different meanings, e.g. patient 'Doctor, doctor, I feel like a pair of curtains.' Doctor 'Well pull yourself together!'

Pun: an amusing use of a word or phrase that has two meanings, e.g. Seven days without water can make one weak - 1 week.

Riddle: a question that is deliberately confusing and usually has a clever or humorous answer, e.g. What is black and white and red all over? Answer an embarrassed zebra.

Sarcasm: a way of speaking or writing that involves saying the opposite of what you really mean in order to make an unkind joke, e.g. in response to someone arriving an hour late, someone says 'Good of you to arrive on time'.

Satire: using humour to expose foolishness, silliness or stupidity through ridicule, e.g. The government has appointed a new minister The Minister for Silly Walks.

A – Z of Poetry and/or Poets

A

W. Allingham (1824 – 1889)

Born in Ballyshannon, in the County of Donegal in Ireland and died in Hampstead in London, England. His ashes are buried at St. Annes' in Ballyshannon.

Robin Readbreast

Good-bye, good-bye to Summer!

For Summer's nearly done;

The garden smiling faintly,

Cool breezes in the sun;

Our thrushes now are silent,

Our swallows flown away,

— But Robin's here in coat of brown,

And scarlet breast-knot gay.

Robin, Robin Redbreast,O Robin dear!

Robin sings so sweetly

In the falling of the year.

Bright yellow, red, and orange,

The leaves come down in hosts;

The trees are Indian princes,

But soon they'll turn to ghosts;

The leathery pears and apples

Hang russet on the bough;

Its Autumn, Autumn, Autumn late,

'Twill soon be Winter now.

Robin, Robin Redbreast,O Robin dear!

And what will this poor Robin do?

For pinching days are near.

The fire-side for the cricket,
The wheatstack for the mouse,
When trembling night-winds whistle
And moan all round the house.
The frosty ways like iron,
The branches plumed with snow,
—Alas! in winter dead and dark,
Where can poor Robin go?
Robin, Robin Redbreast,O Robin dear!
And a crumb of bread for Robin,
His little heart to cheer.

Analysis:

This is a poem in praise of a bird: the robin redbreast.
There are 3 verses of varying lengths which mainly rhyme alternatively. The metre
consists of weak/strong feet with varying numbers per line.

'Good-bye, good-bye to Summer!
For Summer's nearly done;'

Repetition is used for emphasis and to add to the rhythmic pattern for the words
'goodbye' and 'Summer' are repeated in close proximity.

In line 2, the phrase 'Summer is', is contracted to 'Summer's' to assist the rhythmic
flow.

'The garden smiling faintly,'

In this line, the poet uses personification when he says the garden is 'smiling'. This not only brings to mind a sunny pleasant aspect, but it also appeals to the emotions, for we immediately assume happiness when someone smiles.

'Cool breezes in the sun;'

He uses contrast by mentioning cool breezes within close proximity the 'the sun'.

'Our thrushes now are silent,
Our swallows flown away,'

The shape of the poem is enhanced by lines that begin with the same word 'our', emphasizing that other birds, the thrushes and the swallows have left for the winter, whereas the robin is staying. This represents another usage of contrast as a poetic device. Also, the word 'our' makes the birds a greater concern to us – they are 'our' birds rather than more distant birds that we do not relate to.

'— But Robin's here in coat of brown,
And scarlet breast-knot gay.
Robin, Robin Redbreast, O Robin dear!'

It is evident that his poem was written a long time ago because the meaning of the word 'gay' has changed so much, it is rarely used in poetry meaning 'happy' now.

'Robin sings so sweetly'

This line begins with an alliteration 'sings so sweetly', each word beginning with the letter 's'.

'In the falling of the year.'

The use of the word 'falling' is an effective choice, for it has two meanings, falling as in falling down or going away and it may also remind us of 'the fall' the American word for Autumn when the leaves fall.

'Bright yellow, red, and orange,'

The variety of colours in the leaves ('bright yellow, red and orange') enhances the image of leaves falling.

'The leaves come down in hosts;'
'The trees are Indian princes,'
'But soon they'll turn to ghosts;'

We are reminded of the saying 'Indian summer' when the trees are personified as Indian princes so that we imagine them tall, dark, handsome and of full of promise, but they are further personified as turning to ghosts when all the leaves have gone and they appear to have no life in them.

'The leathery pears and apples
Hang russet on the bough;'

The end of summer and the passing of time into autumn is expressed by the way the ripening of the fruit is described. The word 'leathery' is associated with pears and a brand of apple and its colour is combined in the choice of the word 'russet'.

' It's Autumn, Autumn, Autumn late,
Twill soon be Winter now.
Robin, Robin Redbreast,O Robin dear!
And what will this poor Robin do?
For pinching days are near.'

Repetition of the word Autumn adds to the rhythm and message of the verse. Autumn is definitely present and stretching into Winter. In conjunction with the effect of emphasizing a key word by using repetition, the Robin becomes the repeated word emphasized in the verse. The robin is going to have a difficult time in the coldness and deprivation of winter. Food will be scarce – indicated by the description and personification of days as 'pinching'.

'The fire-side for the cricket,
The wheatstack for the mouse,'

These lines follow on from the mention at the end of the previous verse that winter is coming, a time of deprivation and the need for creatures to find food, shelter and warmth. In the first line the words the 'fire-side' and the 'cricket', we immediately imagine we are at home in front of a warm blazing fire and we are reminded of the feelings evoked by Charles Dickens writing in his fairy tale called 'The cricket on the hearth' which is about home and the strong emotions that home evokes. Home is our shelter as the wheatstack is for the mouse.

'When trembling night-winds whistle
And moan all round the house.'

The alliteration of 'winds whistle' and the onomatopoeic words 'whistle' and 'moan' add to atmosphere of a harsh winter. The winds that 'tremble' rather than 'blow' evoke images of how we feel when we are cold – we shiver and tremble. The assonance in 'winds whistle' and 'round the house' contribute to cohesion. The sense of going round is perpetuated for we may immediately recall the way children love going 'round and round' the roundabout, we imagine the wind going round the house again and again.

'The frosty ways like iron,
The branches plumed with snow,'

The roads and paths are frosty and cold and this feeling is exacerbated with the simile 'like iron' which is hard and cold.
The branches are not 'covered' by snow but are 'plumed' bringing to the imagination visions of the lightness and soft coverage of a birds large feathers.

'— Alas! in winter dead and dark,'

The notion of winter is made worse by personifying it as 'dead'. Aligning the word dead' with 'dark' uses alliteration to heighten the effect.

'Where can poor Robin go?
Robin, Robin Redbreast, O Robin dear!
And a crumb of bread for Robin,
His little heart to cheer.'

Repetition of the subject of the poem helps to bring it to a close and focuses on the central message. The poet is concerned for the robin and appeases the reader when food is left out for the bird and 'cheer' the robin's little heart. The use of heart here, infers that it is the soul as well as the body of the robin the author wishes to nurture.

B

Elizabeth Browning (1806 - 1861)

English, born in Durham died in Italy. Married Robert Browning, had one son.

Sonnets from the Portuguese

XLIII

How do I love thee? Let me count the ways.

I love thee to the depth and breadth and height

My soul can reach, when feeling out of sight

For the ends of Being and ideal Grace.

I love thee to the level of everyday's

Most quiet need, by sun and candlelight.

I love thee freely, as men strive for Right;

I love thee purely, as they turn from Praise.

I love thee with the passion put to use

In my old griefs, and with my childhood's faith.

I love thee with a love I seemed to lose

With my lost saints,--I love thee with the breath,

Smiles, tears, of all my life!--and, if God choose,

I shall but love thee better after death.

Analysis:

This poem is, most likely, an expression of the author's love for her husband.

The line structure of the poem shows that it is based on the 14-line form of an Italian sonnet: the first 6 about her personal love, the next two a twist or 'volta' - which carries on speaking about more general love, and then another idea for the final 6 lines, in this case how her love is deep-rooted in the past.

'How do I love thee? Let me count the ways.'

The author is thinking about how to describe the feelings of love she has. She is suggesting that there are many ways in which she could describe her love. Although not explicit, by starting with one of those unfathomable questions, the nature of love, she introduces a poem that is obviously going to be deep, and/or intense, and/or philosophical. She does not intend to list the ways as though they are easily found - she is inferring that she is going to try to describe the nature of her love in as many ways as she can.

This first line is in the expected iambic pentameter of a sonnet that is to continue for most of the rest of the poem. (How do I love thee? Let me count the ways: da-dum da-dum da-dum da-dum da-dum,) When the rhythm changes, as in line 4, so does the subject or feeling being expressed.

'I love thee to the depth and breadth and height
My soul can reach, when feeling out of sight'

These two lines are discussed together because the meaning is extended across them without a pause or break in the speech (enjambment). This gives more strength to her description. Her love is not just deep, wide and high - it is as deep, high and wide as her soul - if her soul could ever be measured in such a way. 'When feeling out of sight' the author is still talking about the soul, indicating that it may an untouchable source/container of her feelings or deep emotions and is neither measurable nor visible.

'For the ends of Being and ideal Grace.'

'Feeling out of sight' from the previous line may also refer to the unreachable goals of the best of mankind to reach a state of perfect existence ('Being') and spirituality (Grace).

'I love thee to the level of everyday's
Most quiet need, by sun and candlelight.'

Again, weight is given to this idea by lengthening it with enjambment. She says she loves him even in the most mundane, everyday activities. Notice that she heightens the language and ideas by using the superlative ('everyday's most quiet need'). Feelings remain high too, for she talks about 'need' rather than mere meaningless activity. Even in the most ordinary or actions there is an expression of the deepest love.

'By sun and candlelight' contains contrasting ideas. The first suggests day and night - the sun providing light in the day, a candle providing light at night. However, these words also emphasize the brightness and strength of her love - both the sun and the candle give light.

'I love thee freely, as men strive for Right
I love thee purely, as they turn from Praise.
I love thee with the passion put to use
In my old griefs, and with my childhood's faith.'

Although these lines may be read using the traditional iambic rhythm (I love thee freely, as men strive for Right') they become more meaningful if the rhythm is changed: (I love thee freely, as men strive for Right'). This alteration provides variety strengthening the effect of fresh ideas. This is made apparent by the use of the comma mid-line.

'I love thee with a love I seemed to lose
With my lost saints,-I love thee with the breath,

Smiles, tears, of all my life!-and, if God choose,
I shall but love thee better after death.'

Repetition of the word 'love' and of the phrase 'I love thee' holds the poem together. The alliteration and tautology (repetition of an idea) of 'lose' and 'lost' strengthens the meaning and feelings evoked from loss. The enjambment regarding the words 'breath, smiles, tears' also helps to make the line cohesive. In the final two lines the poet brings in the notion of an all-knowing being, God, so that we can understand how enormous and powerful her feelings are. The final word 'death' represents the finality of life and strengthens the idea that she believes in an afterlife when her love will remain constant and even stronger.

C

John Clare (1793-1864)

English; married with 6 children; suffered mental illness in later life.

'I am'

I am: yet what I am none cares or knows,
My friends forsake me like a memory lost;
I am the self-consumer of my woes,
They rise and vanish in oblivious host,
Like shades in love and death's oblivion lost;
And yet I am! and live with shadows tost

Into the nothingness of scorn and noise,
Into the living sea of waking dreams,
Where there is neither sense of life nor joys,
But the vast shipwreck of my life's esteems;
And e'en the dearest--that I loved the best--
Are strange-nay, rather stranger than the rest.

I long for scenes where man has never trod;

A place where woman never smil'd or wept;

There to abide with my creator, God,

And sleep as I in childhood sweetly slept:

Untroubling and untroubled where I lie;

The grass below--above the vaulted sky.

Analysis:

'I am: yet what I am none cares or knows,'

I exist, he says. Yet, even though I know I am here, and I am part of the world and people know I exist, no-one wants to know or cares that I am here.

'My friends forsake me like a memory lost;'

His friends have left him; he feels he cannot enjoy the friendship he once had with them. He uses a simile to liken the loss of his friends to a memory, something very distant that happened long ago and is lost to both his and their consciousness. He could also be referring to his own condition - he is starting to lose his memory and recollections of the times he once had with his close friends are now distant or even lost to him.

'I am the self-consumer of my woes,'

He is saying that his troubles are self-contained, within his own thoughts. Only he really knows what he is suffering. His problems 'eat him up' and no one else can really understand what it is like to experience his suffering.

'They rise and vanish in oblivious host,'

At times his problems greatly increase or disappear into the ether of existence where nothing is known, they completely disappear (momentarily) into a place which is kept by a 'Host' or God who holds everything that is or has been known so that the poet's troubles sink into 'oblivion', they are no longer significant in the whole scheme of things.

'Like shades in love and death's oblivion lost;'

He uses another simile to liken the effective loss of his memories of previous heightened experiences, especially those of love, to mere shadows in the world and within in his troubled memory and are doomed to come to an inevitable finality with the loss and obliteration of a person and all that they have held dear to them in death.

'And yet I am! and live with shadows tost'

He uses the conjunction 'and' as well as the word 'yet' to emphasize that even with all of these worries, he does exist, he knows he exists and thus it matters. He knows he is alive although living with troubled, dark memories that are thrown about within his troubled mind.

'Into the nothingness of scorn and noise,'

In his troubled life that has been full of the derision and fuss of others

'Into the living sea of waking dreams,'

In his life as it is, full of wandering thoughts while he is alive, now,

'Where there is neither sense of life nor joys,'

Where he does not really feel alive or appreciates the joy he may have done once

'But the vast shipwreck of my life's esteems;'

His hopes, desires and achievements have fallen to 'wrack and ruin' indicated by the metaphor 'shipwreck'

'And e'en the dearest--that I loved the best-'

Even the people who have been those he has loved the most

'Are strange-nay, rather stranger than the rest.'

Even they seem different, not like they were, even more changed than everyone and everything else

'I long for scenes where man has never trod;'

He wishes he could go to places no one has ever been before, where there is none of the noise and worry of his present situation.

'A place where woman never smil'd or wept;'

He wants to be where he doesn't have to feel or remember the impact of a woman and her emotions and the effect she has or had on his feelings.

'There to abide with my creator, God,'

He wants to finish it all, to go home and return to where he came from to be with God.

'And sleep as I in childhood sweetly slept:'

He is so tired, he wants to rest, to sleep as soundly as he did when only an innocent child.

'Untroubling and untroubled where I lie;'

He wants his worries to cease. He wants to be no trouble to anyone else, nor suffer from the unhappy and anxious thoughts that he is experiencing now. He wants to rest, be still, and unaffected by his problematic thoughts. The similarity of 'untroubling' and 'untroubled' not only support the rhythm of the line, but introduce two different perspectives, that resting, he would not disturb anyone and he would not be disturbed himself.

'The grass below-above the vaulted sky.'

He wants to rest on green fields or 'grass' leading us to imagine him finally at rest on the 'green pastures' from the 23rd psalm - pastures where he can metaphorically rest in the arms of a caring God. Such pastures are more important and on a higher plane than the sky itself. The 'grass' could also refer to his grave. He wishes to die and be free of all his difficulties.

D

John Donne (1572 - 1631)

Born and died in London, England.   Poet, lawyer and priest in the Church of England; a metaphysical poet; married with 10 children; studied at Cambridge and Oxford Universities.

'Death be not Proud'

Death be not proud, though some have called thee
Mighty and dreadfull, for, thou art not soe,
For, those, whom thou think'st, thou dost overthrow,
Die not, poore death, nor yet canst thou kill mee.
From rest and sleepe, which but thy pictures bee,
Much pleasure, then from thee, much more must flow,
And soonest our best men with thee doe goe,
Rest of their bones, and soules deliverie.
Thou art slave to Fate, Chance, kings, and desperate men,

And dost with poyson, warre, and sicknesse dwell,

And poppie, or charmes can make us sleepe as well,

And better then thy stroake; why swell'st thou then?

One short sleepe past, wee wake eternally,

And death shall be no more; death, thou shalt die.

Analysis:

This 'Holy Sonnet 10' is a sonnet (of 14 lines) with a rhyme pattern abba abba cddc ee. Like the English or Shakespearean sonnet, it has 14 lines made up of 3 quatrains (of 4 lines) and a couplet at the end.

The rhyme scheme follows the Italian or Petrarchan sonnet form in the first two quatrains by using the abba form. He then changes to using cddc in the third quatrain and ends with ee in the couplet.

The poem is one long personification of death and addresses 'Death' as though it were a being. The tone is defiant. It is almost as if the poet is saying 'So there!' at the end, 'Put that in you pipe and smoke it!'

John Donne is known as a 'metaphysical' poet and the poem demonstrates this by the way Death is presented as a constant and inventive metaphor - death *is* a self-important, dreadful 'being'.

'Death be not proud, though some have called thee'

Death, you should not be full of your own self-importance, even though many have said you are all powerful and important.

'Mighty and dreadfull, for, thou art not soe,'

You may be thought of as strong and terrifying yet you are not like that at all

'For, those, whom thou think'st, thou dost overthrow,'

Because those whom you believe you have overcome

'Die not, poore death, nor yet canst thou kill mee.'

Don't die, death, nor can you kill me.

'From rest and sleepe, which but thy pictures bee,'

The stillness and unconsciousness that you are seen to cause. Note the internal rhyming within this line of 'sleepe' and 'bee' which helps to hold the poem together.

'Much pleasure, then from thee, much more must flow,'

Sometimes provides just what some people want, and even more advantages come

'And soonest our best men with thee doe goe,'

For as soon as good people die

'Rest of their bones, and soules deliverie.'

Their bones are given peace and their souls are set free.

'Thou art slave to Fate, Chance, kings, and desperate men,'

You are subject to whatever fate, chance, rulers and men at the end of their tether decide. Notice the emphasis on 'slave; and 'Fate' caused by their assonance.

'And dost with poyson, warre, and sicknesse dwell,'

You have to be associated with the nastier side of the world: poison, war and disease.

'And poppie, or charmes can make us sleepe as well,'

We can get rest and peace with drugs just as well

'And better then thy stroake; why swell'st thou then?'

Which are much better than anything you do by striking us dead, so what reason do you have to swell with pride?

'One short sleepe past, wee wake eternally,'

A brief moment of death and then we are resurrected to an eternal life

'And death shall be no more; death, thou shalt die.'

When death will mean nothing, it will not exist, you, death, will die. The repetition of 'death' and the word 'die' summarize the content of the poem and emphasize the message of the whole poem: 'Death, you will die!'

E

T. S. Eliot (1888-1965)

Thomas Stearns Eliot: born in America died in England; married with no children.

Prelude 1

The winter evening settles down
With smell of steaks in passageways.
Six o'clock.
The burnt-out ends of smoky days.
And now a gusty shower wraps
The grimy scraps
Of withered leaves about your feet
And newspapers from vacant lots;
The showers beat

On broken blinds and chimney-pots,

And at the corner of the street

A lonely cab-horse steams and stamps.

And then the lighting of the lamps.

Analysis:

'The winter evening settles down'

The poem is set at dusk. Personification makes the season (winter) appear human by 'settling down' like a person does after they have finished work and gone home to relax. We assume that the day has been busy and energetic as time now slows or 'settles' down.

'With smell of steaks in passageways.'

Alliteration in 'smell of steaks' also creates a sense of the sizzling sound as well as aroma. People start cooking their dinners and we are reminded of this with the poet's reference to the senses – on this occasion the 'smell' of meat. We are reminded that the people live in crowded conditions, as though in a series of flats, their doors leading to passageways which trap the smells of their cooking.

'Six o'clock.'

We are given the exact time in two abrupt words. This shortening of the line focuses us on it and makes it central to all that is happening. People live a humdrum existence with regular unchanged habits and at six o'clock they cook their evening meal.

'The burnt-out ends of smoky days.'

We are reminded of poor conditions in the area and in the street – the words 'burnt out' create an image of burnt-out cigarettes, possibly thrown carelessly on the pavement, while at the same time bringing to mind images of down-trodden people who have been working too hard for too long – they have little energy left even for the mundane things in life – they are 'burnt -out'

'And now a gusty shower wraps'

We are reminded of the cold of winter as the wind and rain swirl around us

'The grimy scraps'

And the dirty remains, of leaves and possibly litter

'Of withered leaves about your feet'

Like the down-trodden poor people, the leaves are withered or dying around us as we walk in the street. Note the internal assonance within the line.

'And newspapers from vacant lots;'

The showery wind also whirls newspapers strewn in empty, people-less plots of land that no-one has either the money or will to do anything constructive with.

'The showers beat'

The rain is strong and attacks.

'On broken blinds and chimney-pots,'

We are reminded of the poverty of the people and their broken lives as their houses only have broken blinds and chimney pots.

'And at the corner of the street'

As we look further, physically and metaphorically, at the corner of the street.

'A lonely cab-horse steams and stamps.' [*sibilance*] [*off rhyme*]

We see a single horse and cab. It is cold so the horse 'steams' and restlessly moves his feet to 'stamp' out the cold. The alliteration of 'st' in 'steams' and 'stamps' brings to mind the hiss of steam and the almost onomatopoeic sound of the horse's feet stomping.

'And then the lighting of the lamps.'

Like a ray of hope we are told how the dusk ends with the bringing of light onto the scene as the street lamps are lit. Again, the use of alliteration in the words 'lighting of the lamp' gives meaningful shape to the line.

F

William Shakespeare (1564-1616)

Very famous English poet, playwright and actor; married with three children.

'A Sea Dirge'

[*assonance →*] [*alliteration 'f' → tone change*]

Full fathom five thy father lies:
Of his bones are coral made:
Those are pearls that were his eyes: [*off rhyme?*]
Nothing of him that doth fade,
But doth suffer a sea change
Into something rich and strange;
Sea-nymphs hourly ring his knell:
Hark! now I hear them,—Ding, dong, bell.

Analysis:

The poem is from Shakespeare's play 'The Tempest' (Act 1 scene 2) sung by the spirit Ariel (who can take either male or female form).

'Full fathom five thy father lies:'

Your father lies all of five fathoms in the deep sea. The alliteration of 'full', 'fathom', 'five' and 'father' and the rhyming of 'five' and 'lies' establishes the line as strong opening

'Of his bones are coral made:'

The length of time the body has been in the sea has turned his bones into coral.

'Nothing of him that doth fade,
But doth suffer a sea change'

His true self shows no change only the changes that the sea has made.

'Into something rich and strange;'

He has been changed into something special, something different.

'Sea-nymphs hourly ring his knell:'

He has become one with the mysterious world in the depths of the sea where 'sea nymphs' or the forces, currents sway and sound a bell, the bell that is rung to announce death.

'Hark! now I hear them,—Ding, dong, bell.'

Listen to the sound of the death bell. Here the common phrase used to describe the sound of a bell: Ding Dong is onomatopoeic as it imitates the sound of the bell.

G

J. Gay (1685-1732)

English; known for writing 'The Beggar's Opera'

'The Butterfly and the Snail'

As in the sunshine of the morn

A butterfly (but newly born)

Sat proudly perking on a rose,

With pert conceit his bosom glows;

His wings (all glorious to behold)

Bedropt with azure, jet, and gold,

Wide he displays; the spangled dew

Reflects his eyes and various hue.

His now forgotten friend, a snail,

Beneath his house, with slimy trail,

Crawls o'er the grass, whom when he spies,

In wrath he to the gardener cries:

'What means yon peasant's daily toil,

From choking weeds to rid the soil?

Why wake you to the morning's care?

Why with new arts correct the year?

Why grows the peach's crimson hue?

And why the plum's inviting blue?

Were they to feast his taste design'd,

That vermin of voracious kind!

Crush then the slow, the pilfering race,

So purge thy garden from disgrace.

"What arrogance!' the snail replied;

'How insolent is upstart pride!
Hadst thou not thus, with insult vain
Provok'd my patience to complain,
I had conceal'd thy meaner birth,
Nor trac'd thee to the scum of earth;
For scarce nine suns have wak'd the hours,
To swell the fruit, and paint the flowers,
Since I thy humbler life survey'd,
In base, in sordid guise array'd.
I own my humble life, good friend;
Snail was I born and snail shall end.
And what's a butterfly?
At best He's but a caterpillar drest;
And all thy race (a numerous seed)
Shall prove of caterpillar breed.'

Analysis:

'As in the sunshine of the morn
A butterfly (but newly born)
Sat proudly perking on a rose,'

It is a sunny day, symbolic for a happy time. A new-born butterfly is resting proudly on a rose. The word 'perking' adds to the feeling of bonhomie it is engendering. He is cheering us up.

'With pert conceit his bosom glows;
His wings (all glorious to behold)
Bedropt with azure, jet, and gold,'

He is cheekily pleased with himself; he is puffed up with pride. His wings are magnificently coloured blue, red and gold.

'Wide he displays; the spangled dew

Reflects his eyes and various hue.'

He spreads his wings out showing off their brilliant colours that are mirrored in his eyes.

'His now forgotten friend, a snail,
Beneath his house, with slimy trail,
Crawls o'er the grass, whom when he spies,
In wrath he to the gardener cries:'

In the meantime, a friend whom he has ignored, a snail, is the opposite: he cowers under his shell, his horrible slippery track creeps across the grass. The butterfly sees him and angrily complains to the gardener.

'What means yon peasant's daily toil,
From choking weeds to rid the soil?
Why wake you to the morning's care?
Why with new arts correct the year?
Why grows the peach's crimson hue?
And why the plum's inviting blue?

Why do you work to rid the earth of weeds? Why get up every morning to look after the garden with new skills to overcome the difficulties of the seasons? Why take so much trouble to grow beautiful red peaches and tempting blue plums?

Were they to feast his taste design'd,
That vermin of voracious kind!
Crush then the slow, the pilfering race,
So purge thy garden from disgrace.

Given a chance, it would eat these carefully grown foods, this pest that eats so much. It would gradually destroy them, this thieving species, so get rid of them, stop them spoiling your garden.

Note the <u>alliteration in 'vermin' and 'voracious', giving substance to the two key words in the line.</u>

"What arrogance!' the snail replied;
'How insolent is upstart pride!

The snail declares how big-headed and rude he is, how stuck-up and conceited!

'Hadst thou not thus, with insult vain
Provok'd my patience to complain,
I had conceal'd thy meaner birth,
Nor trac'd thee to the scum of earth;'

If you hadn't complained and insulted me like this, compelling me to speak up, I would not have told anyone about your humble beginnings, nor told them how you came from the dregs of society.

"For scarce nine suns have wak'd the hours,
To swell the fruit, and paint the flowers,
Since I thy humbler life survey'd,
In base, in sordid guise array'd.'

For only nine days, when the sun has come up every day to make the fruit grow and to help the flowers flourish, I have observed your inferior life, so low and in such foul camouflage.

'I own my humble life, good friend;
Snail was I born and snail shall end.'

I am my own man, I was born a snail and I will always be a snail. This couplet summarizes his belief expressed in the whole poem and the repetition of 'snail' in the final line helps to underline the importance of his existence as a snail.
'And what's a butterfly?'

So, what is a butterfly?

'At best He's but a caterpillar drest;
And all thy race (a numerous seed)
Shall prove of caterpillar breed.''

All you can say is, at best, it is only a caterpillar and all his over-populated species are established as only caterpillars.

H

Seamus Heaney (1939-2013)

Irish born County Londonderry Northern Ireland and died in Dublin; married with three children.

Digging

Analysis only: (due to copyright issues)

Verse 1, line one: The setting of the poem tells us that the poet is about to use his skill - the skill of writing. The repetition of 'my' emphasizes that the poem is his, and expresses his feelings about what is to follow.

Verse 1, line two: The pen is described as 'squat' - not 'fat' - squat already gives a hint of what is to follow. In the process of digging it is easy to imagine the digger squatting down to put his weight underneath the full spade of earth before retrieving it.

Verse 2, line one: We can easily imagine the poet sitting at his window waiting for inspiration and while waiting he hears the digging. We become one with the writer as our attention is moved from the pen to the sound of digging through the window. The image of the window reminds us of the saying: that it is a slice of life, a means by which we can understand life more fully. Even the suggestion of 'a slice of life' that relates to this imagined connection refers to the way the spade 'slices' through the earth. The description of the sound we can hear as 'clean' and 'rasping', provides a contrast. A sound that is clean or clear is hardly 'rasping'. The title has informed us of the content of the poem, so we can easily 'see' the clean marks in the soil and hear the direct single or 'clean' sound as the spade strikes down into the earth. The soil, with its occasional pebbles, can also be easily imagined as it makes the spade 'rasp'. Note the onomatopoeic word 'rasping' which mimics the sound the spade makes against the gravel.

Verse 2, line two: This line confirms our imagined pebbles and we are told that the ground is 'gravelly'. Notice the alliterations in 'spade', 'sinks' and 'gravelly and 'ground'. The words are next to each other, making the alliteration strong and giving the words importance within the line.

Verse 2, line three: We now understand the meaningfulness of the situation for the poet. It is not just anybody digging, it is his father. The poet looks out to his father, appreciating his humbleness and his connection with the earth. His father is the poet's foundation, the salt of the earth, and has his feet firmly on the ground.

Verse 3, line one: An image of a strong, muscled man - his 'rump' straining. This tough, strong man contrasts with the image of flowers, associated with love, beauty and more feminine qualities. This man is not too proud, He willingly tends to beautiful things.

Verse 3, line two: The digger bends down, digs deep into the earth and history reminds the poet that this humble act of digging reflects centuries of an ordinary human activity that helps to create new life. Digging the soil is the first stage in the preparation for planting the food that feeds the generations.

Verse 3, line three: Words 'stooping in rhythm' are themselves 'rhythmical' and create an image of the man bending low making way for potatoes to be planted.

Verse 3, line four: Repetition of the word 'digging' reminds us of what the poem is about and all that it means to the poet.

Verse 4, line one: His boot is well-worn, practical and un-pretty, it is described as 'coarse', meaning it is useful and serviceable for the task of digging, contrasting with the smoother polished boots of city folk. The boot is not 'placed' or 'on' it is described as 'nestled' on the spade. 'Nestled' indicates the love the digger has for the job. It is a comfortable, homely activity for him. The poet's affinity for digging is emphasized by referring to specific terms that describe the spade: the lug and the shaft.

Verse 4, line two: Specific details sharpen the image of the digger 'levering' the spade against his inside knee. He 'levers' the spade, rather than merely leaning it. This suggests the total involvement of the digger, putting his full weight (and by suggestion, his heart,) behind the activity of digging.

Verse 4, line three: Like rooting out evil, he clears the ground of old, useless growths and buries (i.e. pushes) the spade very deep into the soil. The edge of the spade is described as 'bright' suggesting the contrast between brightness and darkness and good and evil.

Verse 4, line four: All the preparation described above is the foundation for establishing new growth, just as his father has provided a secure foundation for the author as he developed throughout his childhood. We are reminded of this when we know that the father scatters the new potatoes that 'we' the author and he had picked. The author is very much involved. The image here reminds us of the sower scattering his seed used in the Bible as a proverb with the seed representing the deeds that people perform.

Verse 4, line five: The feeling of love has been alluded to throughout the poem thus far and is now wholly confirmed in the word 'loving'. The author continually refers to 'us' and 'we'. He is no longer observing from above, he is very much part of the situation and he and his father love handling the potatoes - very much the foundation of the Irish diet for centuries. The potatoes are described as cool, a relief from the heat and sweat created from digging. They are also described as hard, in the sense that they are full, complete and remind us of the stamina and muscley body of the digger.

Verse 5, line six: Throughout the poem there is the underlying belief in the influence of the 'Almighty' - the hand of God, an omniscient figure, behind the sense of continuity over centuries conveyed. Thus reference to God creates a fitting climax. The hand of God is behind it all. This line also takes us down to earth again, as this kind of phrase is used in everyday speech to emphasize how good someone is at something. 'By God he could ...' We are reminded of the experienced nature of the digger, he is described as 'the old man' which again is a common phrase used to describe one's father in the intimate and often loving way of a son.

Verse 5, line seven: This line ties all the thoughts of the verse together in one succinct statement. It is not just the author's father he is thinking of but results from generations back, from his father, and his father before him.

Verse 6, line one: The diligence of both his father and grandfather is emphasized. The author's pride in their achievement is obvious.

Verse 6, line two: 'Toner is the owner of the bog where the men dug the peat.

Verse 6, line three: Again, the author is personally involved. He remembers a simple task he was given.

Verse 6, line four: We imagine the author as a child, handling the bottle carelessly. This is portrayed by mentioning the paper stopper. It is not the stopper that's 'sloppy' - it's the carrier. His grandfather paid him attention immediately.

Verse 6, line five: He drank the milk and wasted no time in stooping down again to continue his digging.

Verse 6, line six: The word 'nicking' is onomatopoeic - we can hear the spade catching the turf.

Verse 6, line seven: This rhythmical line expresses the rhythmical digging and the repetition of 'down' endorses the feeling of digging down deep in the peat.

Verse 6, line eight: The adjective 'good' reminds us of the 'goodness' of these people.

Verse 7, line one: The smell of potato mould reminds us of what the diggers are removing, it is described as 'cold' or dead. More onomatopoeic words, 'squelch' and 'slap', reinforce the sounds of the images presented.

Verse 7, line two: The peat is 'soggy', full of water. The short, sharp alliteration 'curt cuts' brings the rhythm to a halt and emphasizes their abrupt nature.

Verse 7, line three: The poet reminds us that his father and grandfather are his 'roots', their diligence and good work provided him with a good foundation for his own approach to life and work.

Verse 7, line four: The poet says humbly that he can never reach the high standards that his fore-fathers have set. He has no 'spade' - he doesn't have the wherewith all to achieve their great heights.

Verse 8, line one: All he has, he says, by repeating the opening lines, is the pen that he holds in his hand.

Verse 8, line two: He personifies the pen like someone pausing, thinking, resting just as the poet is.

Verse 8, line three: Then he focuses at last and decides to use his instrument as well as he can, hopefully with the same inherent goodness, dedication and diligence as his forefathers.

I

Rudyard Kipling (1865 – 1936)

English poet and story writer, known for his stories for children and about India; married with three children.

If

IF you can keep your head when all about you

Are losing theirs and blaming it on you,

If you can trust yourself when all men doubt you,

But make allowance for their doubting too;

If you can wait and not be tired by waiting,

Or being lied about, don't deal in lies,

Or being hated, don't give way to hating,

And yet don't look too good, nor talk too wise:

If you can dream - and not make dreams your master;

If you can think - and not make thoughts your aim;

If you can meet with Triumph and Disaster

And treat those two impostors just the same;

If you can bear to hear the truth you've spoken

Twisted by knaves to make a trap for fools,

Or watch the things you gave your life to, broken,

And stoop and build 'em up with worn-out tools:

If you can make one heap of all your winnings

And risk it on one turn of pitch-and-toss,

And lose, and start again at your beginnings

And never breathe a word about your loss;

If you can force your heart and nerve and sinew

To serve your turn long after they are gone,

And so hold on when there is nothing in you

Except the Will which says to them: 'Hold on!'

If you can talk with crowds and keep your virtue,

Or walk with Kings - nor lose the common touch,

If neither foes nor loving friends can hurt you,

If all men count with you, but none too much;

If you can fill the unforgiving minute

With sixty seconds' worth of distance run,

Yours is the Earth and everything that's in it,

And - which is more - you'll be a Man, my son!

Analysis:

'If you can keep your head when all about you' *Are losing theirs and blaming it on you,'*

The author is giving advice to his son saying that if you can stop yourself from worrying too much or getting stressed, even though others are upset and are blaming you for all their troubles,

'If you can trust yourself when all men doubt you,'

He continues with his advice: if you can believe in yourself even though no-one else seems to believe in you at all

'But make allowance for their doubting too;'

and you can forgive them, understand their attitude and their lack of trust in you,

 'If you can wait and not be tired by waiting,'

if you can be patient,

'or being lied about, don't deal in lies,'

or even though others are telling lies about you, you can stop yourself from telling lies too

'Or being hated, don't give way to hating,'

or if you are hated by others and you can stop yourself from feeling the same hatred towards them

'And yet don't look too good, nor talk too wise:'

and if you can stop yourself from showing that you are at all better or wiser than them

'If you can dream - and not make dreams your master;'

if you can dream and hope for the future, but not give in to being a permanent dreamer who does not do anything,

'If you can think - and not make thoughts your aim;'

if you can use your brain but not try to aim to become a thinker only, separate from the real world

'If you can meet with Triumph and Disaster'

if you can experience either great success or terrible failure

'And treat those two impostors just the same;'

if you can treat both success and failure the same and not let them go to your head, or ruin your life

'If you can bear to hear the truth you've spoken
Twisted by knaves to make a trap for fools,'

if you can put up with hearing your true words changed by unkind people to influence other foolish people into believing their lies about you

'Or watch the things you gave your life to, broken,'

or you can stand by and watch someone destroy all the good work that you have spent your life doing

'And stoop and build 'em up with worn-out tools:'

and pick yourself up, dust yourself off and start all over again

'If you can make one heap of all your winnings
And risk it on one turn of pitch-and-toss,'

if you can take risks and build on what you have achieved already

'And lose, and start again at your beginnings'

and even though you fail, you can be willing to start all over again.

'never breathe a word about your loss;'

never going on about your failure

'If you can force your heart and nerve and sinew
To serve your turn long after they are gone,'

if you can make yourself work as hard as you can for a better future, long after your enemies have gone

'And so hold on when there is nothing in you'

and persist when you feel you have nothing more to give

'Except the Will which says to them: 'Hold on!''

except the determination in you that says to everyone 'wait', 'hang in there'

'If you can talk with crowds and keep your virtue,'

if you can be friends with a lot of people and still keep to your own principles

'Or walk with Kings - nor lose the common touch,'

or if you can associate with very important people but still sympathise and be part of the normal human race

'If neither foes nor loving friends can hurt you,'

if no- one can hurt you

'If all men count with you, but none too much;'

if everyone is important to you, but not overly too important, if you can keep your own integrity

'If you can fill the unforgiving minute
With sixty seconds' worth of distance run,'

if you can turn a bad minute into a worthy one – making every second count in a positive way'

'Yours is the Earth and everything that's in it,'

you will become master of your world and cope with everything in it

'And - which is more - you'll be a Man, my son!'

and what is more, you will have become the epitome of what it is to be a real man and all that it means.

J

James Joyce (1882 -1941)

James Augustine Aloysius Joyce, born in Dublin died in Zurich; married with two children.

'Strings in the Earth and Air'

Strings in the earth and air
Make music sweet;
Strings by the river where
The willows meet.

There's music along the river
For Love wanders there,
Pale flowers on his mantle,
Dark leaves on his hair.

All softly playing,
With head to the music bent,
And fingers straying
Upon an instrument.

Analysis:

'Strings in the earth and air'

This poem is a personification of love and in this first line just like 'love makes the world go round', the poet refers to the connections love makes with the world as strings that we associate with binding us together. Love is ever-present in the air and in the earth – it is in us and all around us.

'Make music sweet;'

The personification is continued as the poet describes these strings as making life very pleasant by making 'sweet music', just as we use the phrase 'It was music to my ears' when we really liked something.

'Strings by the river where
The willows meet.'

Love is everywhere, even when we walk by the river which we imagine is lined with willow trees.

'There's music along the river'

The idea that love is there by the river is repeated

'For Love wanders there,'

The poet gets to the point and 'love' is named as being the subject of his poem and it is there, present at the riverside.

'Pale flowers on his mantle,'

Love, like the riverbank, is covered in pale flowers

'Dark leaves on his hair.'

Love, like the trees, has dark leaves above, in his hair.

'All softly playing,'

refers to the beauty and gentility of the scene.

'With head to the music bent,'

Love is pictured with his head bent as if in deep thought listening to the beauty of the surroundings.

*'And fingers straying
Upon an instrument.'*

Love is moving lightly as if gently touching the strings of the world, just as we say he touched the strings of my heart.

K

John Keats (1791-1825)

English Romantic poet, never married; died in Rome, Italy.

'The Terror of Death'

When I have fears that I may cease to be
Before my pen has glean'd my teeming brain,
Before high-piled books, in charactery,
Hold like rich garners the full ripen'd grain;
When I behold, upon the night's starr'd face,
Huge cloudy symbols of a high romance,
And think that I may never live to trace
Their shadows, with the magic hand of chance;
And when I feel, fair creature of an hour,

That I shall never look upon thee more,

Never have relish in the faery power

Of unreflecting love;--then on the shore

Of the wide world I stand alone, and think

Till love and fame to nothingness do sink.

Analysis:

This is a sonnet of 14 lines in the English of Shakespearean tradition with lines that rhyme abab, cdcd, efef and end with a couplet (two lines) gg:

When I have fears that I may cease to be (a)

Before my pen has glean'd my teeming brain, (b)

Before high-piled books, in charactery, (a)

Hold like rich garners the full ripen'd grain; (b)

When I behold, upon the night's starr'd face,(c)

Huge cloudy symbols of a high romance, (d)

And think that I may never live to trace (c)

Their shadows, with the magic hand of chance; (d)

And when I feel, fair creature of an hour,(e)

That I shall never look upon thee more, (f)

Never have relish in the faery power (e)

Of unreflecting love;--then on the shore (f)

Of the wide world I stand alone, and think (g)

Till love and fame to nothingness do sink.(g)

The rhythm uses the expected iambic pentameter (five groups of weak-strong stress patterns:

'When I have fears that I may cease to be

However, there are lines that, when reading with this stress pattern, would detract from the meaning. The alteration of the stress pattern causes the reader to pause and brings attention to these lines. They contain some of the most important ideas that the poet wants to reader to focus on e.g. Line 3: 'Before high-piled books in charactery'. Central to the first four lines is the notion that he fears he will not finish the books that would contain his deepest, most effective work.

'When I have fears that I may cease to be'

He begins the line with 'when', creating a sense of incompleteness. He does not say 'I fear' but 'When I fear' - he experiences this on a number of occasions, it is something that others can feel and share too- it is not a single occurrence. 'When' indicates that his ideas will not be resolved until the final sentences - beginning 'then'.

The assonance in this first line holds it together: When I have fears that I may cease to be. The repetition of 'I' emphasizes that the poem reflects feelings about himself. It is about his inner self, the most important part of himself (and the most important part of others).

The word 'may' seems incongruous for it is certain that he will cease to be when he dies. However, 'may' introduces the notion of uncertainty and takes the reader beyond the physical presence to a more high-minded philosophical regime. It suggests that he is talking about the survival of his ideas, rather than his physical body.

'Before my pen has glean'd my teeming brain,'

Again, the use of a preposition ('before') holds the thoughts suspended in a continuous thread. He gives prominence to his 'pen' as though it were the pen and not his own hand that were to write. He alludes to the notion that 'the pen' is mightier than the sword'. 'The pen' is a powerful tool and thus he uses the term here. The word 'glean'd' suggests he is thinking of his best writing - not just all his ideas and possible written items, but the power of his 'pen' selecting from his thoughts the best, most effective words and ideas that he holds in his brain. He has so many thoughts that his brain is described as 'teeming' with them. This gives a sense of urgency, will he have time to express the best of his ideas before he dies?

'Before high-piled books, in charactery,
Hold like rich garners the full ripen'd grain;'

The sense of urgency and continuance is maintained with the use of the preposition 'before' at the beginning again.

The assonance in 'High-piled book's' and the suggestion of a change of rhythm makes these three words important. They bring to mind an image of a large pile of books that Keats may have written, but more figuratively speaking, reflects the idea that Keats's writing is 'high' as in 'high and mighty' - or above others - that is, powerful and packed (or 'piled') with many worthy expressions and ideas.

'In charactery' introduces the suggestion of giving the books character or interest just as people with character are often thought of as more interesting than those who have little 'character'. He thus introduces the notion of personification by giving the books such personal connotations.

The books 'hold' rather than 'contain' his work. The image of a loved one holding another, or someone holding on to something they treasure is brought to mind. The contents are so important that they are held onto, not merely put inside.

He uses a simile to strengthen the images. He likens the gathering together of his best writing to 'rich' or worthy, knowledgeable gatherers (garners) of the staff of life ('grain'), 'grain' that is full (complete, comprehensive) and 'ripen'd' (reached maturity, that is, his ideas and expression have reached their pinnacle of achievement).

'When I behold, upon the night's starr'd face,'

The preposition 'when' is used again as a cohesive device, holding his thoughts together and indicating that he is moving towards a final resolution (at the end?). When he looks up into the heavens, suggesting looking for inspiration, or thinking high thoughts, he sees the starry night, in itself a symbol of love and romance or an awareness of man's insignificance compared to the eternity that the sky or the universe represent. Even the sounds of 't's', 'st' 'd' and 'ce' in 'night's starr'd face' may be said to evoke the impression of bright sharp images of stars against the large expanse of the dark night sky. Note that the sky is personified as having a 'face', a meaningful appearance.

'Huge cloudy symbols of a high romance,'

The most common 'huge' symbol' in the sky is the full moon. This may be referred to as well as clouds that perhaps take the shape of other romantic symbols. The poet is thinking of love.

'And think that I may never live to trace
Their shadows, with the magic hand of chance;'

He regrets that he may never experience even a little or 'trace' of what the clouds or 'shadows' represent. He may never experience the power of a meaningful relationship. The clouds' shadows represent abstract ideas and symbols that remind the viewer of love. It will only be by luck, of the 'magic hand' of chance that will make it possible for the poet to experience true love. Note again, the use of personification when it is not just 'chance' but the 'hand of chance' , as though some superior being has a 'hand' in such chance or luck.

'And when I feel, fair creature of an hour,'

The conjunction 'and' added to the preposition 'when' at the beginning of the line emphasizes the cohesion of the poem. The word 'feel' is isolated to an extent by the addition of a comma which causes the reader to pause, giving strength to the meaning of 'feel' which includes strong senses of emotion.

'Fair creature of an hour' reminds us of the beauty ('fair') and complexity of the focus of his love. His prospective lover is described as a creature, not in the animalistic sense, but as someone enigmatic, 'super' human. The poet is always thinking of her - she is 'of the hour' or he thinks of her hourly - at any hour of the day.

'That I shall never look upon thee more,'

'That' is finally included at last, making the statement powerful: One of the most frightening of his thoughts comes to him - what if he ever believes that he will never experience love or see his prospective lover again?

'Never have relish in the faery power
Of unreflecting love;-then on the shore
Of the wide world I stand alone, and think'

The terrible effect of the possibility of never experiencing or 'relish'-ing love or his prospective lover again is made strong with the repeat of the word 'never'.

The word 'faery' brings supernatural qualities to the power of love, those of magic and woven spells known to 'fairies' often featured in literature.

By describing love as 'unreflecting', it is portrayed as immediate, impulsive, all-giving. To love wholly is to love without any pause for thought, deep emotions and desires are acted upon without reflection.

If he is to die before experiencing any of this, he will really feel desolate and alone, like someone 'shored' up or put on the shelf away from the buzz of humanity. He will be separate from the world, he will be entirely on his own with nothing else to do but to think his own thoughts that he may never be able to share.

'Till love and fame to nothingness do sink.'

The final line is the crunch line. He will be wrapped up in all these high thoughts and feelings and no matter how much love or fame he experiences, even these will disappear into obscurity (sink to nothingness). All his desire to express fully the experience of a great love and of communicating with the world great words and thoughts that evoke such experiences in others - all this will be lost when he dies and he can no longer think.

L

Henry Wadsworth Longfellow (1807-1882)

American; known for writing 'The Song of Hiawatha'; married with 6 children.

'The Wreck of the Hesperus'

It was the schooner *Hesperus*,
That sail'd the wintry sea;
And the skipper had taken his little daughter,
To bear him company.

Blue were her eyes as the fairy flax,
Her cheeks like the dawn of day,
And her bosom white as the hawthorn buds,
That ope in the month of May.

The skipper he stood beside the helm,
His pipe was in his mouth,
And he watch'd how the veering flaw did blow
The smoke now west, now south.

Then up and spake an old sailor,
Had sail'd the Spanish Main,'
I pray thee put into yonder port,
For I fear the hurricane.

'Last night the moon had a golden ring,
And to-night no moon we see!
'The skipper he blew a whiff from his pipe,
And a scornful laugh laughed he.

Colder and louder blew the wind,

A gale from the north-east;

The snow fell hissing in the brine,

And the billows frothed like yeast.

Down came the storm and smote amain

The vessel in its strength;

She shuddered and paused like a frighted steed,

Then leaped her cable's length.

'Come hither! come hither! my little daughter,

And do not tremble so;

For I can weather the roughest gale,

That ever wind did blow.'

He wrapped her warm in his seaman's coat,

Against the stinging blast;

He cut a rope from a broken spar,

And bound her to the mast.

'O father! I hear the church bells ring,

O say, what may it be?"

'Tis a fog-bell on a rock-bound coast!'

And he steered for the open sea.

'O father! I hear the sound of guns,

O say, what may it be?'

'Some ship in distress that cannot liveIn such an angry sea!'

'O father! I see a gleaming light,

O say, what may it be?'

But the father answered never a word,—A frozen corpse was he.

Lashed to the helm, all stiff and stark,

With his face turn'd to the skies,

The lantern gleam'd through the gleaming snow
On his fixed and glassy eyes.
Then the maiden clasped her hands and prayed
That saved she might be;

And she thought of Christ who stilled the waves
On the Lake of Galilee.
And fast through the midnight dark and drear,
Through the whistling sleet and snow,

Like a sheeted ghost the vessel swept
T'wards the reef of Norman's Woe.
And ever the fitful gusts between
A sound came from the land;

It was the sound of the trampling surf
On the rocks and the hard sea-sand.
The breakers were right beneath her bows,
She drifted a dreary wreck,

And a whooping billow swept the crew
Like icicles from her deck.
She struck where the white and fleecy waves
Look'd soft as carded wool,

But the cruel rocks they gored her sides
Like the horns of an angry bull.
Her rattling shrouds all sheathed in ice,
With the masts went by the board;

Like a vessel of glass she stove and sank,
Ho! ho! the breakers roared.
At day-break on the bleak sea-beach,
A fisherman stood aghast,

To see the form of a maiden fair

Lashed close to a drifting mast.

The salt sea was frozen on her breast,

The salt tears in her eyes;

And he saw her hair like the brown sea-weed,

On the billows fall and rise.

Such was the wreck of the *Hesperus*,

In the midnight and the snow;

Heav'n save us all from a death like this,

On the reef of Norman's Woe!

Analysis:

This is a ballad, telling the story of the wreck of the sailing boat named the Hesperus.
The metre is mostly iambic (weak/strong), as expected.

'It was the schooner Hesperus,
That sail'd the wintry sea;'

The scene is set The Hesperus was sailing in the sea at winter.

'And the skipper had taken his little daughter,
To bear him company.'

The captain of the vessel had brought his daughter with him for company.

'Blue were her eyes as the fairy flax,
Her cheeks like the dawn of day,
And her bosom white as the hawthorn buds,
That ope in the month of May.'

His daughter was beautiful, with blue eyes, blond hair, pink cheeks, and her skin as white as the hawthorn buds that open in May. Similes create a stronger image of the daughter. Her cheeks are 'like' dawn, her bosom 'as' white 'as' hawthorn buds.

'The skipper he stood beside the helm,
His pipe was in his mouth,
And he watch'd how the veering flaw did blow
The smoke now west, now south.'

The captain stood with his hands on the ship's wheel, his pipe in his mouth, as he noticed the winds change and blow stronger, the smoke from his pipe being sent in different directions, west and then south.

'Then up and spake an old sailor,
Had sail'd the Spanish Main,'
I pray thee put into yonder port,
For I fear the hurricane.'

Then an experienced sailor who had managed to sail to the American continent and back told the captain to go into port for he knew a hurricane was coming.

'Last night the moon had a golden ring,
And to-night no moon we see!

The old sailor had seen a ring round the moon on the previous evening, and there was no moon to be seen tonight – all signs of bad weather.

'The skipper he blew a whiff from his pipe,
And a scornful laugh laughed he.'

The captain just smoked his pipe and ignored him, laughing sneeringly.

'Colder and louder blew the wind,
A gale from the north-east;
The snow fell hissing in the brine,

And the billows frothed like yeast.'

The wind developed into a gale from the north-east, snow fell into the foamy sea and the clouds filled and raged in the sky. The word 'hissing' is onomatopoeic, like the sound it represents. We can easily imagine the furious sound of the wind and the sea. 'Billows frothed like yeast' is a simile that creates a strong image of the teeming clouds frothing in the sky. The word 'frothing' brings to mind wild animals that 'froth at the mouth' when uncontrollable and angry.

'Down came the storm and smote amain
The vessel in its strength;
She shuddered and paused like a frighted steed,
Then leaped her cable's length.

The storm attacked the boat with all its power. The boat shook and, like a frightened horse, rose up its entire length. Again, the image is enhanced with the simile that likens the schooner to a scared horse.

'Come hither! come hither! my little daughter,
And do not tremble so;
For I can weather the roughest gale,
That ever wind did blow.'

The captain calls his daughter to come to him. He urges her not to be afraid for he is all-powerful, he can overcome the worst winds that ever could blow. The poem expresses the pride of the captain here as he boasts about his capabilities. The moral of the story is told. We are urged to listen further for we fear that the common proverb 'Pride goes before a fall' will become reality here. The urgency of the situation is used by repeating 'come hither'.

'He wrapped her warm in his seaman's coat,
Against the stinging blast;
He cut a rope from a broken spar,
And bound her to the mast.'

As a caring father, he takes off his coat and wraps it round her. He cuts off a piece of rope from part of boom that had been smashed by the storm and ties her to the mast. Contrast makes these lines effective as the poet puts the words 'warm; and 'stinging blast' in close proximity. It takes only two words ('broken spar') to tell us that the boat is breaking up.

'O father! I hear the church bells ring,
O say, what may it be?''

The daughter cries out that she can hear bells that foretell of her death.

'Tis a fog-bell on a rock-bound coast!'
And he steered for the open sea.

He tells her it's only the bell that warns of rocks when there is a fog, so he heads away from them and out to the open sea. Her cries, and her father's answers that dismiss her fears, serve as a question and answer refrain that quite often occurs in ballads.

'O father! I hear the sound of guns,
O say, what may it be?'

The daughter cries that she can hear guns.

'Some ship in distress that cannot live
In such an angry sea!'

Her father dismisses them as distress signals from a ship that is unable to cope with the storm, suggesting that he, the all powerful skipper, is much better than that ship's master.

"O father! I see a gleaming light,
O say, what may it be?''

The daughter cries that she can see a light.

'But the father answered never a word,—A frozen corpse was he.
Lashed to the helm, all stiff and stark,
With his face turn'd to the skies,
The lantern gleam'd through the gleaming snow
On his fixed and glassy eyes.'

Her father didn't reply He was dead. The image is strengthened with the alliteration describing his dead body as 'stiff and stark'. The guttural letter 'g' used in the last two lines: 'gleamed, gleaming and glassy' heightens the dark meaningful mood.

'Then the maiden clasped her hands and prayed
That saved she might be;
And she thought of Christ who stilled the waves
On the Lake of Galilee.'

The maiden prays. She wishes Jesus would come and tell the storm to stop just as he stopped the storm when he was on the lake of Galilee. The word maiden, reminds us of how young and vulnerable his daughter is. Her prayer and the mention of Jesus help us realize that death is near.

'And fast through the midnight dark and drear,
Through the whistling sleet and snow,
Like a sheeted ghost the vessel swept
T'wards the reef of Norman's Woe.'

This dark, furious storm, pushes the boat rapidly towards the reef called Norman's Woe, a dangerous reef off Massachusetts in America. The alliteration of single syllabled words 'dark and drear' not only helps the rhythmic urgency of the verse, but brings to mind, albeit obliquely, her forthcoming death. The onomatopoeic word 'whistling' is enhanced with the following alliteration in 'sleet and snow'.

'And ever the fitful gusts between

A sound came from the land;
It was the sound of the trampling surf
On the rocks and the hard sea-sand.'

The tale is made even more tragic as we learn that, between the gusts of the storm, there are moments of quiet when the sound of the surf on the sandy shore could be heard and we know that they very nearly made it. The repetition of 'sound' emphasizes this key word as does it alliteration with 'sea-sand.'

'The breakers were right beneath her bows,
She drifted a dreary wreck,
And a whooping billow swept the crew
Like icicles from her deck.'

The waves picked up the remnants of the boat and, in one big thrust, pushed the dead crew off its deck into the sea. The simile that likens the dead bodies of the crew to icicles leaves a chilling effect, the substance of the ballad.

'She struck where the white and fleecy waves
Look'd soft as carded wool,
But the cruel rocks they gored her sides
Like the horns of an angry bull.'

The boat finally pulled up where the waves were gentle and soft but the evidence was there that the rocks had stuck into the boat and wrecked it. The first two lines contrast well with the second two. The alliteration of the gentle sound of 'w' in 'white', 'waves' and 'wool', and the simile comparing the waves to wool that has been cleaned and smoothed, endorse the tranquillity expressed.

'Her rattling shrouds all sheathed in ice,
With the masts went by the board;
Like a vessel of glass she stove and sank,
Ho! ho! the breakers roared.'

The ship smashed to pieces and sank. The waves laughed at their success. The onomatopoeic word 'rattling' reminds us of the rattle of skeletons. The phrase 'by the board' reminds us of its figurative meaning that they are insignificant, unimportant or are now worthless. The simile likening the boat to a glass enhances the image of it shattering into tiny pieces. In the final line, the waves are personified and, like a human destroyer, roar with evil laughter.

'At day-break on the bleak sea-beach,
A fisherman stood aghast,
To see the form of a maiden fair
Lashed close to a drifting mast.'

When the sun comes up a lone fisherman is shocked to find the dead body of the young girl lashed to a mast as it drifts by in the water. The use of 'k' in break and bleak add to the hardness of the message. The assonance in 'bleak sea' and 'beach' strengthens the effect. This verse uses contrast too: The terrible scene is contrasted with the image of the vulnerability of the young, fair haired girl.

'The salt sea was frozen on her breast,
The salt tears in her eyes;
And he saw her hair like the brown sea-weed,
On the billows fall and rise.'

She had been overcome by the salty sea and her hair was wet and dark as her body moved up and down in the waves. The repetition of 'salt' enhances the harshness of the situation. Her 'salt tears' strengthens the sadness. The inertness of her body is emphasized by the word 'frozen' – not only is she cold but she is completely still. Her hair that had been previously described as fair and by implication, beautiful, is now unattractive, spoiled by the sea expressed clearly in the simile as it is likened to 'brown sea-weed'. The word 'weed' brings to mind unwanted, unpleasant items in the garden.

'Such was the wreck of the Hesperus,
In the midnight and the snow;

Heav'n save us all from a death like this,
On the reef of Norman's Woe!'

These words bring the ballad and the moral of the story to an end. 'Heav'n save us all from a death like this' implores us to take note and to avoid anything like this ever happening again.

M

John Milton (1608-1674)

English; married with four children.

'Song on May Morning'

Now the bright morning star, day's harbinger,
Comes dancing from the east, and leads with her
The flow'ry May, who from her green lap throws
The yellow cowslip, and the pale primrose.
Hail, bounteous May, that doth inspire
Mirth and youth and warm desire!
Woods and groves are of thy dressing,
Hill and dale doth boast thy blessing.
Thus we salute thee with our early song,
And welcome thee, and wish thee long.

Analysis:

'Now the bright morning star, day's harbinger,'

Venus appears – a bright star in the east that heralds the new day.

'Comes dancing from the east, and leads with her
The flow'ry May, who from her green lap throws

The yellow cowslip, and the pale primrose.'

The star shines, as if 'dancing'. The poet personifies the star as a bright, new, and cheerful influence that brings May which, in turn, is personified as if a being that brings an abundance of greenery, and flowers especially the yellow cowslips and pale primroses.

May's 'green lap' reminds us of a mother holding her child on her knee – a symbol of love and affection.

Hail, bounteous May, that doth inspire
Mirth and youth and warm desire!

Welcome May when everything thrives, and happiness and youthful desires are inspired.

Hill and dale doth boast thy blessing.
Thus we salute thee with our early song,
And welcome thee, and wish thee long.

You (May personified) are welcomed everywhere up hill and down dale so we salute you with our newly inspired singing. We welcome May and wish it to last for a very long time.

N

Thomas Nashe (1567-1601)

English poet, writer of controversial material.

'Spring, the sweet Spring'

Spring, the sweet Spring, is the year's pleasant king;

Then blooms each thing, then maids dance in a ring;

Cold doth not sting, the pretty birds do sing,

Cuckoo, jug-jug, pu-we, to-witta-woo!

The palm and the may make country houses gay,

Lambs frisk and play, the shepherds pipe all day,

And we hear aye birds tune this merry lay,

Cuckoo, jug-jug, pu-we, to-witta-woo.

The fields breathe sweet, the daisies kiss our feet,

Young lovers meet, old wives a sunning sit,

In every street these tunes our ears do greet,

Cuckoo, jug-jug, pu-we, to-witta-woo.

Spring, the sweet Spring.

Analysis:

This is a poem in praise of Spring.

Spring, the sweet Spring, is the year's pleasant king;
Then blooms each thing, then maids dance in a ring;

Sweet Spring is here, the loveliest time of the year when everything grows and blossoms and young girls dance round the Maypole in a ring.

The repetition of 'Spring' emphasizes the importance of the keyword. Spring is personified as a 'king'. We know it is the best time of year, just as we a king rules over his kingdom. Everything blossoms, including young girls.

Cold doth not sting, the pretty birds do sing,
Cuckoo, jug-jug, pu-we, to-witta-woo!

It is not cold now, we are not suffering from winter's freezing temperatures. All the birds sing. We hear the sound of the birds, the cuckoo, the nightingale, which makes the sounds 'jug-jug' and 'pu-we' and the tawny owl whose call sounds like 'to-witta-woo'. These words are more than onomatopoeia, they are made-up words that try to imitate exactly the call of the birds. This final line acts as a refrain to the other verses.

The palm and the may make country houses gay,
Lambs frisk and play, the shepherds pipe all day,
And we hear aye birds tune this merry lay,
Cuckoo, jug-jug, pu-we, to-witta-woo.

Palm tree fronds and the mayflower or hawthorn blossom brighten up houses in the country. Lambs are born and frolick in the meadows where shepherds play their pipes all day. We can hear the birds joining in the song with their calls: 'Cuckoo'...

The fields breathe sweet, the daisies kiss our feet,
Young lovers meet, old wives a sunning sit,
In every street these tunes our ears do greet,
Cuckoo, jug-jug, pu-we, to-witta-woo.

The lush meadows smell sweet, our feet in the lush grass are touched by daisies. Young love thrives and the old women come out into the sunshine to sit. In every street we can hear music, the music that represents spring especially the bird calls: 'Cuckoo ...'

O

Wilfred Owen (1893-1918)

Wilfred Edward Salter Owen MC; English poet and soldier, known for his poetry about WW1; born Shropshire, died Sambre-Oise canal France.

'Anthem for a doomed youth'

What passing-bells for these who die as cattle?
Only the monstrous anger of the guns.

Only the stuttering rifles' rapid rattle

Can patter out their hasty orisons.

No mockeries now for them; no prayers nor bells;

Nor any voice of mourning save the choirs,

The shrill, demented choirs of wailing shells;

And bugles calling for them from sad shires.

What candles may be held to speed them all?

Not in the hands of boys, but in their eyes

Shall shine the holy glimmers of good-byes.

The pallor of girls' brows shall be their pall;

Their flowers the tenderness of patient minds,

And each slow dusk a drawing-down of blinds.

Analysis:

This is an anthem or song of celebration, or in this case, a song in commemoration.

'What passing-bells for these who die as cattle?'

What bells are rung out to announce the deaths of those who died ignominiously, like slaughtered animals. The simile that represents the soldiers as animals emphasizes the contempt with which they are treated.

'Only the monstrous anger of the guns.
Only the stuttering rifles' rapid rattle
Can patter out their hasty orisons.'

Only the heinous hatred of weapons, only the rat tat tat of the machine guns can spell out their spontaneous pleadings and prayers. The repetition of 'only' emphasizes the monstrosity of it all. The alliteration in 'rapid rattle' gives an onomatopoeic reference to the sound of the guns.

No mockeries now for them; no prayers nor bells;
Nor any voice of mourning save the choirs,

The shrill, demented choirs of wailing shells;
And bugles calling for them from sad shires.

There are no hypocrites paying homage to them now, no prayers are said for them and no church bells are rung. No person speaks of their sad loss. The only voices that speak of their plight is the loud, mad noise of whining bombs, and bugles calling them to rise to the battle from the heart-breaking places where they have died. The repeated negative words, 'no', 'no' and 'nor' make the horror of the situation more noticeable. Repetition of 'choirs' reminds us that the guns are shot by groups of people, that in a sense we are all guilty of ignoring the plight of these people who die uncared for.

What candles may be held to speed them all?

What lights or church candles will be lit to help them on their heavenly journeys?

Not in the hands of boys, but in their eyes
Shall shine the holy glimmers of good-byes.

It is not the young choirboys in church who will shine forth and reflect their brief and hurried thoughts of farewell.

The pallor of girls' brows shall be their pall;
Their flowers the tenderness of patient minds,
And each slow dusk a drawing-down of blinds.

The shocked pale faces of their girlfriends will be their only coffin covers. The girls' wreaths the only sign of the appreciation of their gentle, tolerant characters who have been treated so badly and, every evening as the sun sets, people close their eyes to the dreadfulness of this situation. The alliteration in 'dusk and drawing- down' help to create a feeling of slowing down so much that unless there is change this attitude will remain for eternity.

P

Edgar Allen Poe (1809 – 1849)

American born in Boston died Baltimore; married with no children.

'Sonnet – Silence'

There are some qualities- some incorporate things,

That have a double life, which thus is made

A type of that twin entity which springs

From matter and light, evinced in solid and shade.

There is a two-fold Silence- sea and shore-

Body and soul. One dwells in lonely places,

Newly with grass o'ergrown; some solemn graces,

Some human memories and tearful lore,

Render him terrorless: his name's "No More."

He is the corporate Silence: dread him not!

No power hath he of evil in himself;

But should some urgent fate (untimely lot!)

Bring thee to meet his shadow (nameless elf,

That haunteth the lone regions where hath trod

No foot of man,) commend thyself to God!

Analysis:

This is similar to a Shakespearean sonnet of 14 lines, (although this poem consists of 15 lines) containing verses of 4+5+4+3 lines rhyming abab, cddcc, efef, ee.

'There are some qualities- some incorporate things,

That have a double life, which thus is made

A type of that twin entity which springs

From matter and light, evinced in solid

and shade.'

There are some attributes that are integrated within our society, that have a double existence and as such comes of both substantial bodies as well as more spiritual entities.

'There is a two-fold Silence- sea and shore
Body and soul. One dwells in lonely places,
Newly with grass o'ergrown; some solemn graces,
Some human memories and tearful lore,'

Both the body and the soul comprehend the silence engendered by the more moveable sea of life and the more solid basis of the shore. Silence can be found in places where no-one has been, some in heart-felt spiritual powers from God and some in the more traditional emotions engendered by memories people have of distressing moments in their lives.

'Render him terrorless: his name's "No More."
He is the corporate Silence: dread him not!
No power hath he of evil in himself;
But should some urgent fate (untimely lot!)
'Bring thee to meet his shadow (nameless elf,'

He - 'silence' named death – becomes something that should not be feared. He is the strength that comes from the fact that everyone meets him. Death is not bad in itself, it should not be feared and if death comes unexpectedly and early -

That haunteth the lone regions where hath trod
No foot of man,) commend thyself to God!'

This nameless entity, found in uninhabited areas where no man has (comprehended ?) before, then you should put yourself in your Maker's care.

Q

William Shakespeare (1564-1616)

Very famous English poet, writer of plays and actor; married with three children.

Queen Mab (abridged)

O then, I see, Queen Mab hath been with you.

She is the fairies' midwife, and she comes

In shape no bigger than an agate stone

On the fore-finger of an alderman;

Drawn with a team of little atomies

Athwart men's noses as they lie asleep:

Her wagon spokes made of long spinner's legs:

The cover, of the wings of grasshoppers;

The traces, of the smallest spider's web;

The collars of the moonshine's watery beams;

Her whip of cricket's bone, the lash, of film;

Her wagoner, a small grey-coated gnat,

Not half so big as a round little worm,

Pricked from the lazy finger of a maid:

Her chariot is an empty hazel nut,

Made by the joiner squirrel, or old grub,

Time out of mind the fairies' coachmakers.

And in this state she gallops night by night,

Through lovers' brains, and then they dream of love;

On courtiers' knees that dream on court'sies straight;

O'er lawyers' fingers, who straight dream on fees;

O'er ladies' lips, who straight on kisses dream.

Analysis:

The effect of this poem is created, more than anything, by Shakespeare's careful choice of words that bring to mind a host of images, adding to the literal meaning of the single words or phrases.

'O then, I see, Queen Mab hath been with you.'

Oh, I see that Queen Mab has already been with you

*'She is the fairies' midwife, and she comes
In shape no bigger than an agate stone
On the fore-finger of an alderman;'*

She helps give birth to all the fairies (or 'dreams'), appearing in a form smaller than a gemstone you would find worn by a politician.

By referring to the Queen as 'midwife' Shakespeare gives the impression that she is more than ruler of the fairies (or 'dreams'), she is intimately involved in their creation. In describing her diminutive size Shakespeare expresses the tremendous power she has by saying she is smaller than the tiny stone worn by people associated with power in human society.

*'Drawn with a team of little atomies
Athwart men's noses as they lie asleep:
Her wagon spokes made of long spinner's legs:
The cover, of the wings of grasshoppers;
The traces, of the smallest spider's web;
The collars of the moonshine's watery beams;
Her whip of cricket's bone, the lash, of film;
Her wagoner, a small grey-coated gnat,
Not half so big as a round little worm,
Pricked from the lazy finger of a maid:'*

Her chariot is pulled by a group of tiny creatures the size of atoms that cross men's noses while they lay sleeping. Her wagon wheels are made of spiders' legs, the cover of grasshopper wings, and the harness of tiny cobwebs. The necks of creatures pulling the chariot are collared with pale moonbeams. Her whip is a bone from a cricket, the thong of her whip a thin membrane. Her coachman is a small biting insect in a grey jacket and he is smaller than a little roundworm picked off the finger of a slothful maid.

Human-kind is reduced to insignificance in comparison with her power. This is expressed by having her tiny chariot being able to crawl across the very noses of men, while they remain perfectly unaware in their sleep. Her wagon wheels are small but strong, just as spiders' legs are thin but strong. The strength of grasshopper wings are belied by their appearance and also help form her chariot. The moon and all its inherent influence on the world is involved in shaping the Queen's chariot as moonbeams form around the necks of the 'horses'. Cobwebs, though thin are also strong, the insect is not benign, it has the power to hurt by biting, just as Queen Mab has power. By referring to the roundworm, a parasite on the human body,

Shakespeare endorses the propensity for evil the Queen has by introducing something that is considered evil and nasty. The reference to wickedness is continued as the image of a slothful servant is brought forth.

On courtiers' knees that dream on court'sies straight;
O'er lawyers' fingers, who straight dream on fees;
O'er ladies' lips, who straight on kisses dream.

She rides over courtiers' knees as they dream of favours given to them. She rides over lawyer's fingers that dream of huge amounts of money and she rides over the lips of ladies who dream of kisses.

Shakespeare brings into the speech some of the most despicable members of society: courtiers who bow and scrape hypocritically at court to gain favour and lawyers who only want to get money out of their clients. By implication, she thinks nothing (by riding over) ladies who are perhaps idle therefore fat and unattractive who can only dream of kisses.

R

Christina Georgina Rossetti (1830-1894)

English; never married.

'Remember'

Remember me when I am gone away,

Gone far away into the silent land;

When you can no more hold me by the hand,

Nor I half turn to go yet turning stay.

Remember me when no more day by day

You tell me of our future that you plann'd:

Only remember me; you understand

It will be late to counsel then or pray.

Yet if you should forget me for a while

And afterwards remember, do not grieve:

For if the darkness and corruption leave

A vestige of the thoughts that once I had,

Better by far you should forget and smile

Than that you should remember and be sad.

Analysis:

This poem is a sonnet of 14 lines, with the rhyming pattern similar to a Shakespearean sonnet in that the verses appear to consist of 4+4+4 lines with a couplet at the end. Although it does not follow the expected rhyming pattern exactly, the last two lines form a couplet in meaning and each of the first groups of 4 lines begin with the same meaningful word 'Remember'.

On the other hand, the sonnet may also be said to fall into a similar shape to that of an Italian and/or Petrarchian sonnet, and can be grouped into a set of 8 lines (an octet) following a traditional abba,abba pattern, followed by a sestet (a group of six lines) which has its own distinct rhyming pattern cdd,ece.

'Remember me when I am gone away,'

The poet asks to be remembered after she had died. The enormity and impact of death is emphasized by the euphemism for dying: 'gone away'.

'Gone far away into the silent land;'
When you can no more hold me by the hand,'

She will go into a place where there is nothing, no sound, where her lover cannot touch her or express affection by holding her hand.

Again, the euphemism for dying (gone far away) is repeated thus emphasizing its significance.

'Nor I half turn to go yet turning stay.'

Where she is going, she will not be able to show her love for him in those tiny gestures that mean so much, like half turning to go but being reluctant to leave and turning back again to stay with him after all.

The repetition of the word 'turn' underlines the importance of the word to the emotions portrayed.

'Remember me when no more day by day
You tell me of our future that you plann'd:'

Remember me even though you can no longer sit with me every day and talk to me of the future that you have charted for us.

The poem is about remembering, and beginning a line that is important to the structure of the poem with the repeated word, 'remember' centres the line and the whole message of the poem.

Use of the phrase 'day by day' not only emphasizes the loss of their time together every day, but the phrase itself gives a sense of habit and timelessness.

'Only remember me; you understand
It will be late to counsel then or pray.'

Just remember me, just think of me for it will be too late to discuss anything with me or to pray for something different.

The use of the word 'understand' conveys more than the lover being asked to understand that she is only asking him to comprehend what she means by 'remember' - she is also asking him to be aware that she will indeed have gone and will not be there for him to talk to in the same way as before.

'Yet if you should forget me for a while
And afterwards remember, do not grieve:
For if the darkness and corruption leave
A vestige of the thoughts that once I had,'

In a more forgiving tone, the poet forgives him in advance if he does forget her for a moment and then suddenly remembers her and feels guilty. She tells him not to worry if the dark void that her loss creates leaves only a tiny reflection of the deep thoughts and feelings she once had.

'Better by far you should forget and smile
Than that you should remember and be sad.'

It would be much better if he should be happy, even if it means forgetting her, than it would be if he remained sad by remembering her.

This couplet summarizes the whole message of the poem – remember me but not at the expense of your own happiness. Contrasts form the basis of this couplet:

between happiness and sadness represented by 'smile' and 'sad' (alliterations) and remembering and forgetting. The most important of these two words, 'remember',s mentioned in the important final utterance.

S

Percy Bysshe Shelley (1792-1822)

English Romantic and lyric poet; born in England, died in Italy. Married twice with three children.

'The Widow Bird'

A widow bird sate mourning for her love
Upon a wintry bough;
The frozen wind crept on above,
The freezing stream below.
There was no leaf upon the forest bare,
No flower upon the ground,
And little motion in the air
Except the mill-wheel's sound.

Analysis:

This poem is one long metaphor for life. The world is a desolate place when you have lost your loved one. Even though you feel the world has frozen still and there is no life in it anymore, life goes on like the turning of the millwheel.

'A widow bird sate mourning for her love'
Upon a wintry bough;'

A bird that had lost its mate sat sadly on a cold tree branch in winter.

'The frozen wind crept on above,

The freezing stream below.'

The icy wind blew on in the sky above, and the stream below grew colder.

There was no leaf upon the forest bare,
No flower upon the ground,
And little motion in the air
Except the mill-wheel's sound.

The forest was bare, there were no flowers, the air was still and all that could be heard was the turning of the millwheel.

T

Alfred Tennyson (1809-1892)

English born in Somersby, Linconshire, died Aldworth UK. Poet Laureate, married with two sons; a lord.

'The Charge of the Light Brigade'

HALF a league, half a league,
Half a league onward,
All in the valley of Death
Rode the six hundred.
'Forward, the Light Brigade!
Charge for the guns! ' he said:
Into the valley of Death
Rode the six hundred.

'Forward, the Light Brigade! '
Was there a man dismay'd?
Not tho' the soldier knew
Some one had blunder'd:

Their's not to make reply,

Their's not to reason why,

Their's but to do and die:

Into the valley of Death

Rode the six hundred.

Cannon to right of them,

Cannon to left of them,

Cannon in front of them

Volley'd and thunder'd;

Storm'd at with shot and shell,

Boldly they rode and well,

Into the jaws of Death,

Into the mouth of Hell

Rode the six hundred.

Flash'd all their sabres bare,

Flash'd as they turn'd in air

Sabring the gunners there,

Charging an army, while

All the world wonder'd:

Plunged in the battery-smoke

Right thro' the line they broke;

Cossack and Russian

Reel'd from the sabre-stroke

Shatter'd and sunder'd.

Then they rode back, but not

Not the six hundred.

Cannon to right of them,

Cannon to left of them,

Cannon behind them

Volley'd and thunder'd;

Storm'd at with shot and shell,

While horse and hero fell,

They that had fought so well

Came thro' the jaws of Death,

Back from the mouth of Hell,

All that was left of them,

Left of six hundred.

When can their glory fade?

O the wild charge they made!

All the world wonder'd.

Honour the charge they made!

Honour the Light Brigade,

Noble six hundred!

.

Analysis:

This poem tells the story of a true tragic event when the British cavalry of over 600 men were led by Lord Cardigan against the Russians in the Battle of Balaclava in the Crimean War in 1854. Bad communication from the leaders meant that the Light Brigade was sent in the wrong direction against insurmountable odds. Many were killed and injured and the brigade had to retreat.

'HALF a league, half a league,

Half a league onward,

All in the valley of Death

Rode the six hundred.

'Forward, the Light Brigade!

Charge for the guns! 'he said:

Into the valley of Death

Rode the six hundred.'

'Charge!' was the order even though the enemy were over a mile away. The cavalry soldiers rushed into the valley where they were certain to die.

The rhythm of the poem moves on and on taking the action forward. Words and phrases are repeated like the rhythm of horses in gallop. Reference to the Valley of Death reminds us of the 23rd psalm from the Bible which says that no matter how bad things are, God is with you he will support you. ('Even though I walk through the valley of the shadow of death, I will fear no evil because you are with me ... you comfort me') Here, it helps express the idea that no matter how bad the situation was, something good would come from it – the bravery of the men will never be forgotten.

'Forward, the Light Brigade! '
Was there a man dismay'd?
Not tho' the soldier knew
Some one had blunder'd:
Their's not to make reply,
Their's not to reason why,
Their's but to do and die:
Into the valley of Death
Rode the six hundred.'

Without question, the brigade charged forward. Even though the soldiers knew it was a mistake, who were they to question an order? They were ordered to attack so, bravely, they charged ahead, every one of the six hundred of them.

The momentum of the movement of the soldiers charging on horseback is maintained in the repetitive pattern of the lines: 'Their's ...'.

The last two lines form the refrain that sums up the enormity of the tragedy.

'Cannon to right of them,
Cannon to left of them,
Cannon in front of them
Volley'd and thunder'd;
Storm'd at with shot and shell,
Boldly they rode and well,

Into the jaws of Death,
Into the mouth of Hell
Rode the six hundred.'

Even though they were surrounded by cannons and gunfire, they courageously charged forward even unto death. The refrain is altered slightly so that they rode into 'the mouth of Hell' something more horrendous than the Valley of Death for now they were in the midst of mayhem where they were being slaughtered.

'Flash'd all their sabres bare,
Flash'd as they turn'd in air
Sabring the gunners there,
Charging an army, while
All the world wonder'd:
Plunged in the battery-smoke
Right thro' the line they broke;
Cossack and Russian
Reel'd from the sabre-stroke
Shatter'd and sunder'd.
Then they rode back, but not
Not the six hundred.'

They took out their sabres and brandished them and charged, killing some of the gunners, even though everyone knew that this was a huge mistake. They went straight into the smoke from the guns, they broke through the line of Russians, and fought hand to hand with their sabres and then, broken, the few rode back.,

The repeated word 'flashed' expresses the sheer determination of the cavalrymen. Even in certain defeat, there was fire in them yet. The final line alters the refrain by shortening it to a brief, blunt statement. The shortened line represents the shortening of the lives and the depletion of the number of men remaining alive.

'Cannon to right of them,
Cannon to left of them,

Cannon behind them

Volley'd and thunder'd;

Storm'd at with shot and shell,

While horse and hero fell,

They that had fought so well

Came thro' the jaws of Death,

Back from the mouth of Hell,

All that was left of them,

Left of six hundred.'

Still under fire from cannons and guns all round them, they fought on even though horses and men fell. They had fought so well and bravely, but only a few survived to return.

The galloping rhythm is maintained in the opening lines here and as the verse continues the rhythm slows until we are faced with the knowledge that there only a few left of the 'six hundred'.

'When can their glory fade?

O the wild charge they made!

All the world wonder'd.

Honour the charge they made!

Honour the Light Brigade,

Noble six hundred!'

The tremendous bravery of these men will never fade even though everyone knew they were doomed because of the incompetency of their leaders. Whatever the reason, it is the courage of these men that should be admired.

The final three lines form orders for us to honour the men, to honour all of these brave 'six hundred'.

Samuel Taylor Coleridge (1772-1834)

English; born Ottery St. Mary UK; died Highgate UK; He and William Wordsworth established the Romantic movement; was a member of the Lake District Poets; was married with 3 children.

'Choral song of Illyrian peasants'

Up! up! ye dames, ye lasses gay!

To the meadows trip away.

Tis you must tend the flocks this morn,

And scare the small birds from the corn.

Not a soul at home may stay:

For the shepherds must go

With lance and bow

To hunt the wolf in the woods to-day.

Leave the hearth and leave the house

To the cricket and the mouse:

Find grannam out a sunny seat,

With babe and lambkin at her feet.

Not a soul at home may stay:

For the shepherds must go

With lance and bow

To hunt the wolf in the woods to-day.

Analysis:

Illyria is the name given to the western part of the Balkan peninsula in ancient times. In those days, wolves roamed the land.

Up! up! ye dames, ye lasses gay!

To the meadows trip away.

Tis you must tend the flocks this morn,

And scare the small birds from the corn.

Not a soul at home may stay:

For the shepherds must go

With lance and bow

To hunt the wolf in the woods to-day.

The poet exhorts the people to run to the meadows to guard the sheep and shoo away the birds from the corn. No one must stay at home for the shepherds have to go to hunt and kill the wolf.

The iambic rhythm of the opening line mimics running which adds to the urgency of its call. The final line is a refrain that summarises what must happen.

Leave the hearth and leave the house

To the cricket and the mouse:

Find grannam out a sunny seat,

With babe and lambkin at her feet.

Not a soul at home may stay:

For the shepherds must go

With lance and bow

To hunt the wolf in the woods to-day.

You must leave, find a comfortable safe place in the sun for granny, and the baby and little lamb. No-one should stay at home, for the shepherds must hunt and kill the wolf.

The regular rhythm of the first line again mimics running and reflects the urgency of the situation. This verse uses repetition to enhance the rhythm and make the message stronger by repeating the word 'leave'. The alliteration of 'hearth' and 'house' in this line makes it even stronger and more effective.

V

John Moultrie (1799-1874)

English; born London; died Rugby UK (of smallpox caught from a parishioner); Ordained as a priest lived at parsonage in Rugby; was married with 3 sons and 4 daughters.

'Violets'

Under the green hedges after the snow,
There do the dear little violets grow,
Hiding their modest and beautiful heads
Under the hawthorn in soft mossy beds.
Sweet as the roses, and blue as the sky,
Down there do the dear little violets lie;
Hiding their heads where they scarce may be seen,
By the leaves you may know where the violet hath been.

Analysis:

Under the green hedges after the snow,
There do the dear little violets grow,
Hiding their modest and beautiful heads
Under the hawthorn in soft mossy beds.
Sweet as the roses, and blue as the sky,
Down there do the dear little violets lie;
Hiding their heads where they scarce may be seen,
By the leaves you may know where the violet hath been.

This poem consists of simply rhyming couplets that reflect the simplicity of the lowly violet and is homage to this humble flower which comes out in spring after winter and the snow has finished. They are not easy to see amongst their more conspicuous leaves.

The poem personifies the violet as though it has human qualities of shyness and modesty. Their flowers are called 'heads' and they lie in 'beds'. A simile enhances the imagery and likens the violet to the sweetness of roses and the blueness of the sky.

W

William Wordsworth (1770-1850)

Famous English Romantic poet; married with five children.

'Daffodils'

I wandered lonely as a cloud

That floats on high o'er vales and hills,

When all at once I saw a crowd,

A host, of golden daffodils;

Beside the lake, beneath the trees,

Fluttering and dancing in the breeze.

Continuous as the stars that shine

And twinkle on the milky way,

They stretched in never-ending line

Along the margin of a bay:

Ten thousand saw I at a glance,

Tossing their heads in sprightly dance.

The waves beside them danced; but they

Out-did the sparkling waves in glee:

A poet could not but be gay,

In such a jocund company:

I gazed--and gazed--but little thought

What wealth the show to me had brought:

For oft, when on my couch I lie

In vacant or in pensive mood,

They flash upon that inward eye

Which is the bliss of solitude;

And then my heart with pleasure fills,

And dances with the daffodils.

Analysis:

This is a lyric poem written after the poet and his sister came across a spectacular dell of daffodils when they were in the Lake District (UK).

'I wandered lonely as a cloud
That floats on high o'er vales and hills,'

The poet was walking slowly absorbed in his own thoughts. In a famous simile, he likens his high spirits to a cloud high above the land. The poem is in iambic tetrameter, a short syllable is followed by a long or stressed syllable four times. The rhythmic regularity of this poem adds to its appeal.

When all at once I saw a crowd,
A host, of golden daffodils;

The poet sees a lot of daffodils. He personifies them as a 'crowd' and a 'host'. He exaggerates the colour by calling them 'golden' rather than plain 'yellow'.

The assonance between 'host' and 'golden' helps with the cohesion of the line.

'Beside the lake, beneath the trees,
Fluttering and dancing in the breeze.'

They are next to the lake and under the trees moving in the breeze. The alliteration of 'beside and beneath' helps add to the already appealing structure.

He exaggerates the movement of the flowers by personifying them as 'dancing'. The word 'fluttering' appeals to the sense of hearing as it brings to mind the gentle sound that plants can make in a breeze.

'Continuous as the stars that shine
And twinkle on the milky way,'

They are grouped together in a long unbroken line. The poet uses an exaggerated simile to liken this line of flowers to the brilliance of the stars of the Milky Way.

'They stretched in never-ending line
Along the margin of a bay:'

They extend along the edge of the bay. Here the idea of the heavens is extended by describing the line is 'never-ending', it is infinite.

'Ten thousand saw I at a glance,
Tossing their heads in sprightly dance.'

There were so many of them and they were moving in a delightful way. Common to most lyrical poets, hyperbole is part of his technique. He says there are 'ten thousand' of the flowers, but it is quite unlikely that he actually counted them. He simply means there were a lot. The daffodils are personified again as we imagine them 'tossing their heads' in a lively 'dance.'

'The waves beside them danced; but they
Out-did the sparkling waves in glee:'

The water of the lake was ruffled by the breeze but this was nothing compared to the beauty of the daffodils. The waves are personified for effect too.

'A poet could not but be gay,
In such a jocund company:'

A poet cannot help but be happy in such joyful company.

'I gazed--and gazed--but little thought
What wealth the show to me had brought:'

He looked and looked but never thought what pleasure the display would bring him. The repetition of 'gazed' gives the impression of the poet standing and looking at the daffodils for a very long time. The alliteration in 'what wealth' adds to the appeal of the verse.

'For oft, when on my couch I lie
In vacant or in pensive mood,'
They flash upon that inward eye
Which is the bliss of solitude;'
And then my heart with pleasure fills,
And dances with the daffodils.'

Often, when he is lying on his couch, day-dreaming, the image of these daffodils flashes into his mind and he relives the special feelings of solitude and joy he experienced before.

X

Hồ Xuân Hương (1772-1822)
Vietnamese poet; never married.

'Autumn Landscape'

Drop by drop rain slaps the banana leaves.
Praise whoever sketched this desolate scene:

the lush, dark canopies of the gnarled trees,
the long river, sliding smooth and white.

I lift my wine flask, drunk with rivers and hills.
My backpack, breathing moonlight, sags with poems.

Look, and love everyone.
Whoever sees this landscape is stunned.

Analysis:

'Drop by drop rain slaps the banana leaves.'

The poet immediately sets the scene. We can see the large dark green banana leaves, we know we are in a hot country and we can hear the drops of rain as they make a sound on the leaves.

The poet immediately appeals to our senses. He uses onomatopoeic words to represent the sound of the rain. The words 'drop' and 'slap' represent exactly the sound the rain makes when it falls on the leaves.

'Praise whoever sketched this desolate scene:'

Pay homage to the creator of this solitary picture. The word 'sketched' gives the impression that the poet's view has been specially drawn.

'The lush, dark canopies of the gnarled trees,
the long river, sliding smooth and white.'

He describes some of the detail of what he sees. The trees twisted with age. Their long branches create a covering of dark green leaves. He uses alliteration to describe the river as 'sliding' and 'smooth' which strengthens the image of the water shining as it moves slowly along.

'I lift my wine flask, drunk with rivers and hills.
My backpack, breathing moonlight, sags with poems.'

We imagine the poet gazing at this scene, sipping wine taken from the flask in his backpack. In lyrical style, he exaggerates his feelings, relating the wine to his feeling drunk with so much beauty. His backpack is part of him, inspired by the moonlight and full of poetry that this experience has awakened.

'Look, and love everyone.
Whoever sees this landscape is stunned.'

Anyone who sees this scene will be as amazed as he is. His exhortation to 'look and love' is strengthened with the alliteration within it.

Y

William Butler Yeats (1865-1939)

Irish; born in Ireland died in France.

'A Poet to his Beloved'

I bring you with reverent hands
The books of my numberless dreams;
White woman that passion has worn
As the tide wears the dove-gray sands,
And with heart more old than the horn
That is brimmed from the pale fire of time:
White woman with numberless dreams
I bring you my passionate rhyme.

Analysis:

This is a lyrical poem by Yeats to a woman he had loved for years. Her name was Maude Gonne, an actress and political activist who led an interesting and varied life.

'I bring you with reverent hands

The books of my numberless dreams;'

Yeats brings all his hopes and dreams throughout countless years to her

'White woman that passion has worn
As the tide wears the dove-gray sands,'

He writes of her purity of heart and of the way the passing years have softened youthful passion.

A <u>simile</u> is used that <u>compares the tide</u> wearing down the sand on the shore to the huge length of time that it has taken to <u>soften her passion</u>. The tide, or life, has aged her. The choice of the words 'dove-gray' gives the impression that she has changed, the colour being softer than the bright yellow that sand is usually associated with. Symbolism suggests that sands refer to the sands of time and 'dove' a symbol of love.

'And with heart more old than the horn
That is brimmed from the pale fire of time:'

Her love has known much <u>depth and experience</u> and made her the person she is, a person who has been made complete by a constant all-consuming passion even though its brilliance has softened over time.

Important words, 'heart' and 'horn' <u>are emphasized by use of alliter</u>ation.

'White woman with numberless dreams
I bring you my passionate rhyme.'

Woman with the purest of ideals, I bring you my heart-felt poem. The strength of her ideals and her womanhood are emphasized by the alliteration in 'white woman'. The endless strength of her ideals is expressed in 'numberless dreams'.

Z

Thomas Hardy (1840- 1928)

English; his ashes are buried in Poet's corner, Westminster Abbey.

Zermatt to the Matterhorn

Thirty-two years since, up against the sun,
Seven shapes, thin atomies to lower sight,
Labouringly leapt and gained thy gabled height,
And four lives paid for what the seven had won.

They were the first by whom the deed was done,
And when I look at thee, my mind takes flight
To that day's tragic feat of manly might,
As though, till then, of history thou hadst none.

Yet ages ere men topped thee, late and soon
Thou watch'dst each night the planets lift and lower;
Thou gleam'dst to Joshua's pausing sun and moon,
And brav'dst the tokening sky when Caesar's power
Approached its bloody end: yea, saw'st that Noon
When darkness filled the earth till the ninth hour.

Analysis:

'*Thirty-two years since, up against the sun,*'

Hardy commemorates a climbing accident that happened some 32 years ago, when seven climbers battled against the sun to try to reach the summit of the Matterhorn. The subtle alliteration of since, against and sun add to rhythmic flow of the line which varies according to the emphasis needed to highlight key words. The word 'against' suggests the struggle that they had and how hot the sun was.

'Seven shapes, thin atomies to lower sight,'

They were seven insignificant bodies at the bottom of the Matterhorn, a huge mountain in the European Alps. The alliteration of 's' is continued, the climbers are de-personalised into insubstantial figures. When they started off from the bottom of the mountain, they were not of any significance.

'Labouringly leapt and gained thy gabled height,'

With their hard work they managed to reach the top. Alliteration of 'labouringly', 'leapt' and 'gabled' add to the flow and cohesion, while their tremendous feat is highlighted by the two contrasting words together: 'labouringly' and 'leapt'. 'Labouringly' suggested slow, tedious, hard work, while 'leapt' suggests the great height of achievement they made in successfully reaching the summit. From this line onwards the poet personifies the Matterhorn addressing it as though it were human by the use of 'thy'.

'And four lives paid for what the seven had won.'

But after success came failure , as four of the seven climbers died on the way down. The blunt statement that includes the numbers: four and seven with the contrasting ideas of the way the four paid with their lives for the success of the seven gives the line shape and emphasises the magnitude of the event.

'They were the first by whom the deed was done,'

They were the first people to achieve this goal. The rhythm changes at the end of the line to the more common and effective iambic structure (weak strong) 'by whom the deed was done' emphasizing the importance of the deed.

'And when I look at thee, my mind takes flight'

And when the poet looks at the Matterhorn, his mind is overcome, he is over-awed. The iambic pattern is continued.

'To that day's tragic feat of manly might,'

By that day's tragic event and of such brave, strong men. The courage and strength of the climbers is expressed in the alliteration 'manly might'..

'As though, till then, of history thou hadst none.'

It was as though the Matterhorn had never had any importance until then. .The iambic pattern is maintained so includes the historical form 'hadst', and the two short words 'hadst none' at the end of the line underline the difference now, when the Matterhorn and the men's their deed have become famous.

'Yet ages ere men topped thee, late and soon'

Over the years men have managed to scale your heights. The word 'topped' not only refers to reaching the summit but creates an impression that this massive alp has been beaten.

'Thou watch'dst each night the planets lift and lower;'

The Matterhorn has seen the planets come and go. Again alliteration in 'lift and lower' the placement of these two opposing concepts close together creates cohesion and strengthens the effect.

'Thou gleam'dst to Joshua's pausing sun and moon,'

The Matterhorn has understood the power of Joshua when he stopped the sun and moon in their tracks until his nation Israel had avenged its defeat by Egypt. The line is permeated with reference to light in the word 'gleam'dst', 'sun' and 'moon' suggesting an image of the Matterhorn as it is lit up by the different heavenly bodies of the sun and moon, while the personification is strengthened by using the word 'gleam' and one can have a 'glimmer' of an idea. The alp has tremendous awareness and understanding.

'And brav'dst the tokening sky when Caesar's power'
Approached its bloody end: yea, saw'st that Noon'
When darkness filled the earth till the ninth hour'.

You knew the heavenly activity when Caesar's power came to a bloody end, when he was murdered by Brutus and his friends, and you know that day when darkness overcame the earth   after Jesus died. These lines compound the tragic circumstances of the death of the climbers, and also create a very strong impression of very powerful mountain in body and in spirit. The personification is paramount.

This list of poets and poems is only gives you a taste.

Preparation for examinations:

In preparation for your exams, set yourself questions that ask you to compare and contrast poems or poets.

If one particular poem or poet interests you, do some research on that poem or poet as you are more likely to remember, and be able to use, information that interests you. You can use the information you remember to bring into your discussion on an unseen poem in your examination – e.g. 'like Keats, this poet …' or 'this particular line reminds me of … but this poem uses more modern language, for example ...'

When you are writing your answers for your examinations, all the points you make should be supported with evidence from the poems. For example, it is not enough to say 'The poem is a ballad'. You need to provide evidence from the poem to support this, for example: 'The poem is a ballad for it tells a story, a story that is based on a folk tale/legend/ myth. It is easy to imagine it as a song and, as in most ballads, it is about love.'

Finally, most important of all, enjoy your poetry experience!

Rosemary Westwell

rjwestwell@hotmail.com

 The author is Australian-born teacher and writer Dr Rosemary Westwell who lives in Cambridgeshire, England. She moved to the UK in 1971. After a varied career with a number of different jobs, including selling bikinis in Harrods, and working in Madame Tussaud's, she finally settled with her British husband in Cambridgeshire, teaching in a number of different schools in the county. After the birth of the second child, her husband began to show signs of an illness that degenerated into dementia and he is now permanently in a care home. She has five university degrees (in music, the arts and education) and completed her PhD in 2007. She has two daughters and a growing number of grand children who live in the UK.

The author gives light-hearted talks about her experiences as an Australian-born citizen establishing a new life in the UK and about her difficulties of learning Spanish after acquiring a flat in Spain. She directs a choir called *The Isle Singers* which gives concerts on a regular basis and continues to teach English, Piano and Singing in Cambridgeshire.

Her PhD thesis is available free on: http://eprints.ioe.ac.uk/48/

Other publications:

available on www.amazon.com:

'Out of a Learner's Mouth' a humorous account of her language learning experiences in Spain 'Teaching Language Learners' a book of suggestions and ideas for teaching languages

'Twenty Tips for Teaching IGCSE ESL'

'The Spelling Game'

She has also written 'John, Dementia and Me', a semi-autobiographical novel based on the true story of her husband's decline with dementia, available on www.northstaffordshirepress.com and from August 2014, on www.amazon.com

'Spontaneous Survival Lessons in English' and

'Activities to Engage with The Woman in White and The Lady in the Lake' have been published by ZigZag Education. http://zigzageducation.co.uk

Printed in Great Britain
by Amazon